ATTRACTION MARKETING

ATTRACTION MARKETING

How To Attract All The Perfect Clients You Want

ANNIE MEACHEM

LEANMARKETING™
★PRESS★

First Published In Great Britain 2005
by Lean Marketing™ Press
www.leanmarketingpress.com

Typeset in Garamond and Humanist.

To Sam – for being ever the catalyst

Acknowledgements

I'd like to thank the following people for their assistance and support with the production of this book and the journey that it documents:

My family, Peter, Sam and Joanna for their love and support.

My clients, each of whom brought me a lesson to learn.

My coaches and physical guides on the journey: Elizabeth Ferguson, Dr John Stevenson, Ginny Baillie and Georgina Woudstra.

Jo Losack, for her inspirational ideas. Maggie Gudmundsson, for introducing me to my spiritual guides for the journey.

Coach University USA, for their great training, and to the work of the late Thomas Leonard for first introducing me to Attraction.

Debbie Jenkins and Joe Gregory of Lean Marketing Press (*www.BookShaker.com*) for making the book publishing process feel effortless.

All of those members of the coaching community and my local business networks who so generously helped me with information, ideas and encouragement – too many to mention individually, but to each of you, thank you.

Annie Meachem, 2005

Contents

Do What You Love & Let Attracting Clients Take Care of Itself – Almost!

For some people, it dawns on them gradually…

For others, it's the result of a careful weighing up of the pros and cons…

And for others it comes as a true eureka moment…

What am I talking about?

The moment when you realise what work it is you really want to do. Not just a job done to earn money, or to pass the time, but the work that we pour our hearts and souls into. The work we're passionate about.

For many of us, we want to be defined by our chosen profession; we want to be known as a designer, a therapist, a consultant, whatever our calling is.

My eureka moment happened in 1999… I was idly reading a magazine article about a new profession that had been developed in the USA a few years previously, and in that instant I realised that what I wanted to be was a life coach. It made immediate sense. All my previous work and life experience had unwittingly equipped me to do exactly that!

So I became a student again, and after a couple of years training, I was an official life coach. Fully trained, knowing I was qualified and had the expertise and the necessary qualities to be a wonderful coach, really making a difference in people's lives. I'd practiced my skills with a couple of guinea pig clients throughout my training years and I was ready to go.

Who did I want to coach? – anyone!

What did I want to coach them on? – anything!

Where would I find people who could benefit from and pay me to coach them? – not a clue…

And so my journey of discovery began, a journey that has taken me four years of research and experimentation, of "lucky" encounters and wrong alleys. I now have a system for attracting all that I need and want into my life, and am using it, combined with proven marketing and motivation techniques, to attract all the perfect clients I want to work with too.

So what you have before you is a 30 step programme that will guard you against the feelings of frustration and fear that you don't have enough clients, and you don't really know how to find them.

You won't have to spend lots of your precious time and efforts on activities like selling and marketing. You'll simply be able to spend your days doing the work that you truly love while getting new clients takes care of itself…

Who's This Book For?

This book is for you if you're not naturally drawn to or comfortable with selling and marketing. It's designed for people, just like me, who would rather be spending their time and energy doing what they really love.

If a fairy god–mother had said to me four years ago that she could wave a magic wand and clients would just appear magically, would I have taken her up on it? You bet I would! The bad news is, I'm not a fairy god–mother. Nor do I have a magic wand. The good news is that what I'm about to share with you will enable you to do the things needed so that clients and customers find you, rather than you striving to find them. I'll help you reach a point where you have a constant stream of the right number of the right clients heading your way with a process that feels effortless and easy.

How Do You Simply Attract Clients?

As I said I'm not a fairy go–mother so if you're expecting a "magic wand" approach to doing this, or you want to know the one activity to transform your marketing then I'd suggest you read no further. The reality is that whenever you are designing something, whether it's building a business or putting up a shelf it works best if you approach it holistically, with the end firmly in mind. An unplanned piecemeal approach tends to leave you with less than spectacular results. Well, exactly the same principle applies when you're developing an attraction marketing system. If you make sure to give attention to each of the areas that make up the whole while keeping your focus firmly on what you'd like to achieve, it'll bring you the greatest rewards.

Your Outer Actions & Your Inner World

I'll be introducing you to four different areas that will need your attention and efforts as you design your own attraction marketing system.

These are:

1. The Practical Work – giving you the marketing knowledge you need to devise and maintain a winning marketing system.

2. The Motivational Work – 'your attitude determines your altitude' – this section ensures you're flying high.

3. The Inner Work – allowing you to ensure that your inner world is working in alignment with your actions, rather than unwittingly sabotaging them.

4. The Attraction Work – showing you how to become more 'attractive', so that you can magnetise the success you'd like and draw it into your life.

Can You Have One Area Without The Others?

You may be thinking that all you want to know about is marketing techniques, so why bother with the other stuff? Or that you already know about advertising but can't understand why the clients aren't coming to you.

In all honesty, you can know all the marketing techniques there are, work hard at implementing them, and you will get clients – and the price you often pay is constant hard work and struggle. This costs you, in both financial and personal energy terms. Looking at and developing the other areas will turn your actions into a seemingly effortless approach, giving you more energy to spend where you want to spend it.

Similarly, you may say that you have undertaken a mass of personal development work, and feel that you are already attractive, so why should you be bothered with knowing about marketing techniques? I remember one creative designer saying that if people love his work, they will find him regardless, so he doesn't need to market himself at all. This has an element of truth to it, and yet he'll still need to be able to pay the bills. I'll show you how you can maximise the process by knowing how to make yourself visible to your ideal clients through activities that are enjoyable and rewarding.

So, if you're ready to start designing your own Attraction Marketing System, let's get going!

Chapter One – A Very Good Place To Start…

The very beginning is a very good place to start, so in this section we're going to assess exactly where you are right now in terms of being ready to build a fully functioning attraction marketing system.

Below is a series of 30 statements for you to tick – tick them only if the statement is always true for you.

- ❑ I am in a position of 'visibility' to my ideal clients
- ❑ I am very clear about the benefits I offer my clients
- ❑ I can explain these benefits succinctly and memorably to people I meet
- ❑ I know exactly which clients I can help the most and why
- ❑ I am aware of my unique selling point in my marketplace
- ❑ I add additional value to all my clients
- ❑ I have a basic understanding of selling skills
- ❑ I can identify my ideal client and have a clear picture/description of them
- ❑ I know what I want my business to be like in 1, 3 and 5 years time
- ❑ I have a written marketing plan
- ❑ I set goals and targets for my business marketing and review them regularly
- ❑ I monitor results regularly and adjust my marketing plan accordingly
- ❑ I allocate regular planning time to my marketing
- ❑ I take consistent, persistent action on my marketing to avoid the yo–yo effect
- ❑ I know how I will feel about my business in 1, 3 and 5 years time
- ❑ I know my own strengths and am proud and grateful for them
- ❑ I take responsibility for my actions and for my outcomes

- ❑ I know my areas of weakness and am taking steps to strengthen these
- ❑ I am comfortable with asking for support in areas where it's required
- ❑ My actions are not limited in any way by my fears
- ❑ I have let go of my limiting beliefs
- ❑ My work is an expression of who I truly am
- ❑ I have a positive attitude to life
- ❑ I am able to look for the gift in difficult situations
- ❑ I am grateful for all the good things in my life, large and small
- ❑ I only do work that I feel good about and marketing that I enjoy
- ❑ I look out for synchronicities
- ❑ I respond to opportunities
- ❑ I listen for and act on my intuitive hunches
- ❑ I create a regular number of quiet spaces in my life for reflection or meditation

______ Total Ticked

How many did you tick? Please make a note of the number and the date and keep it somewhere safe. Over the coming pages as you implement the various concepts you'll be introduced to, I'd ask you to go back and update your score. In the meantime, whatever the number you ticked today, please just stop a moment and feel grateful for all that you are achieving already.

You have now identified your present reality, and this lets you be really clear about where the gap lies between where you are now and where you want to be, with a fully functioning attraction marketing system. Once you know the gap between your starting point and your destination, you can start to plan and take the steps that will close that gap, enabling you to effortlessly attract all the clients you want.

When I began discovering this process, I was all too aware of the gap between where I was then and the point of having a successful business. I could answer yes to just two of the statements above.

Firstly, I did know that my work was an expression of who I truly was, I was very clear that I had found the perfect work for me.

Secondly, I knew where my weaknesses lay. Like most people, I knew exactly what I was no good at doing but had little clue at that time about my true strengths. And one thing I knew I didn't know was how to find clients. And so I set about discovering how not only to find clients but have clients find me.

Chapter Two – The Practical Work – What Do You Offer?

In chapter One, you found your starting point for designing your personal attraction marketing system by answering the questionnaire and establishing your baseline score. You're now ready to start taking the actions that will increase that score and enable you to attract all the perfect clients you want.

An important point to note – if you read this book and don't do the exercises or answer the questions, you'll hopefully have increased your knowledge of marketing and success attraction techniques – but this won't make the slightest bit of difference to your end results. Just reading is not enough, you have to take action in some way to start the attraction process rolling.

As you've probably already noticed, there were 30 questions in chapter one – that's one question per step!

So, let's get started. Here are the first questions from the questionnaire, which are all about what you offer to your clients. If you were able to wholeheartedly answer yes to any of them then that's great. If not then the explanation and action steps below each one will help you move to a yes.

Step 1. I am in a position of 'visibility' to my clients

You can be amazingly talented at what you do, you can provide fantastic service, you can have all the other parts of your attraction marketing system in place but that won't mean a thing if you're not 'visible' in some way or other to your ideal clients. You really are expecting miracles if you want them to just find you without so much as a signpost.

The action required is to deliberately 'shine a light' on yourself and your services in a way that is comfortable for who you are at the moment.

Attraction in Action:

1. Brainstorm all the ways you can think of for making you and your services visible. This list might include advertising, networking, speaking, writing, promotional events, direct contact, and many, many others. Just write down anything you can think of. You might like to get friends and family to help you with this.

The idea of this exercise is to come up with as many ways as possible for being 'visible' to your potential clients, some of which will probably be totally daft. Don't censor them at all as you're making the list. You might be tempted to think, "I hate public speaking, so that's out for me", or "Well, I'd never ride through my local town naked on horseback, so that's a non–starter". Don't. Put it on the list anyway. This sort of creative thinking often leads you to ideas that you would never have thought of initially, and can be good fun to do.

2. Refine your list. Look at each activity on your big list and consider how comfortable you feel with undertaking it. If you shy away from it, how could you modify the activity to bring it within your comfort zone? (Comfort zones grow naturally as you grow, so why force

yourself to do something you loathe?) You might feel you could never enjoy public speaking, but maybe would feel comfortable talking to a group of, say, 6. You could then host a lunch for 6 people and just let them know what you offer. Let your imagination run free with all the possibilities, rather than being limited by what you feel you can't do. However, if you really feel you can't face a particular activity in any form, just cross it out and forget it, there are plenty of other ways of getting visible!

3. You now have a list of possible ways for meeting your future clients but before you rush out and action any of them I'd encourage you to work through steps 2–9 first.

With service businesses, where you are selling your skills and time rather than a product that people can pick up and handle, people are buying you, they want something that they think you have to offer them. To be most successful you need to enable them to feel they have got to know you in some way. Then they can begin to build up their trust in you to the point where they're comfortable to buy your service.

One of my clients, Selina, a mobile beauty therapist, was becoming despondent because she'd left leaflets about her services in many different locations, and hadn't had much response. She is an exquisitely beautiful lady and many potential clients who meet her can't help but hope that some of her elegance and glamour will rub off on them! But that can be hard to pick up just from a leaflet. So all Selina had to do instead was find ways of meeting as many people as possible and telling them what she does, letting them see who she is.

Another of my clients, Mark, is a painfully shy but very talented garden designer, who was really struggling to find enough clients to survive. His own garden however was outstanding, so we decided that the best way he could become visible to his ideal clients was to offer his garden as the venue for various coffee mornings, evening galas and other fund raising events attended by the types of people who would be likely to invest in his design services. He then didn't need to market his services, his garden did it for him.

I personally tried using various leaflets, and adverts in local doctors' surgery magazines, but had little response. Not surprising really at a time when the majority of the public had no idea what coaching was or how it could help them. I also wrote to 100 people I knew, letting them know what I was doing, and got three responses that turned into business. On reflection I'll admit that I was still fighting against becoming truly, personally, visible; I wanted to hide behind the leaflets and the mail shots. I was avoiding talking to people in the flesh. I wasted a lot of time and missed many opportunities!

Eventually I realised that I had to meet with real live people and tell them how I could help them – I had to 'network'. But I was really resistant to talking with what I perceived as the impenetrable clusters of the 'men in grey suits' who seemed to inhabit the networking meetings I'd been to in the past. To say it felt well outside of my comfort zone would be an understatement. I was also resistant to the idea of getting up at ungodly hours to attend breakfast meetings, with the added torture of the enforced sixty second speech each week. Ugh!

To make networking work for me, I decided to set up my own networking group. It was for women, it met for supper (not breakfast!) once a month, and no–one was forced to say anything to the group except for their name and what they did – "I'm Julie and I'm an Independent Financial Adviser" was all that was asked of them. I ran it for two years, during which time I met several hundred local businesswomen, many of whom I still keep in touch with now. While I gained some clients from it directly, the amount of business I gained through third party referrals and joint ventures was more than worth the effort. I'd expanded my own comfort zone and ended up, a few years later, joining a breakfast meeting and getting to know those men in grey suits – they didn't bite after all!

Step 2. I am very clear about the benefits I offer my clients

When someone asks you what you do, what they are really wondering is "What can you do to help me?" The typical answer to their question, especially for people who are uncomfortable with marketing, is to say, "I'm a... (insert your profession here)". If, at this point, the other person is still listening, you might then go on to explain how you do it, how you were trained, how much you enjoy it and how it works. All interesting to you but likely to put the average listener to sleep, dreaming of how to escape! People generally do not want to know anything about how you do what you do but everyone likes to know what's in it for them.

So you need to turn the focus away from you and details and onto your client and the big picture. This holds true whether you're talking to them personally, writing words for your website or sending an email.

Attraction in Action:

1. Write down what you do and all the features of your service.

2. Consider each feature and work out the various ways in which that benefits your clients.

3. Keep this list of benefits in a prominent place, become really familiar with it and refer to it as the basis for all your marketing communication.

Sara is an interior designer, so her list of features reads:

1. I come and talk with you, the client, to find out what you want the room to do.
2. I show you a portfolio of styles.
3. I design the room.
4. I draw up plans, 3D drawings and mood boards.
5. If required, I source all the materials.
6. I can also find and supervise all the tradespeople needed to complete the project.

The above is a list features. But we want to pull out the benefits to the customer. We need to answer the question, "Why would I be willing to pay for that?" So let's look at each feature of Sara's business and turn those features into benefits.

Feature 1. I come and talk with you, the client, to find out what you want the room to do.

✓ *Benefit 1:* You get clarity on exactly what you want the room for, thus making sure it does everything you want.

✓ *Benefit 2:* You are prompted to think about practical factors you might not have thought about without my help, thus avoiding expensive mistakes and omissions.

✓ *Benefit 3:* You gain from my experience of having done this for other people – you'll end up with a more versatile use of space with my help than if you'd done it on your own.

✓ *Benefit 4:* You gain from my objectivity, as I have no emotional ties to you, your children, or to your husband, mother–in–law or whoever else might be an influence on your decisions.

Feature 2. I show you a portfolio of styles.

- ✓ *Benefit 1:* You get clarity on what you like, often by discarding those things that you definitely don't like, thus ending up with a finished room or house that you're really delighted with.
- ✓ *Benefit 2:* You gain from my design ability and extensive professional training and experience, thus giving you a far more stylish result than the safe option you may have stuck with or diverting you away from your wilder excesses involving leopard skin print, tacky stencils and sticky back plastic.

Feature 3. I design the room.

- ✓ *Benefit 1:* Again, you gain from my ability to create a unified design that is aesthetically pleasing and harmonious, rather than a mishmash of decoration, thus you can feel confident that the result will be stunning.
- ✓ *Benefit 2:* You're sure that all the details have been thought about, so that the room ends up as planned, rather than having to be compromised later.
- ✓ *Benefit 3:* You end up living in a space that makes you feel really happy.
- ✓ *Benefit 4:* I can turn your the dreams you have in your head into a polished reality.

Feature 4. I draw up plans, 3D drawings and mood boards.

- ✓ *Benefit 1:* Very few non–designers can visualise a finished project in 3D colour in their heads – the 3D drawings help you be sure that what you're going to get is what you want before work begins.
- ✓ *Benefit 2:* Often you don't know what you want until you see it. This way you can fine tune before getting stuck in.

- ✓ *Benefit 3:* You'll save money on buying the wrong decorative items or having to redecorate half way through.

Feature 5. If required, I source all the materials.

- ✓ *Benefit 1:* Do you know how much time it would take you tracking down all the right materials or decorative items? I know just where I can get them before I even include them in your design. This saves you hours.
- ✓ *Benefit 2:* You'll end up with just the right shade of colours, rather than having to compromise because your local stockist hasn't got quite what you wanted.
- ✓ *Benefit 3:* The materials will all be with you or your decorators at an agreed date, rather than you having to wait to get on with the project because you haven't had time to source something vital.

Feature 6. I can also find and supervise all the tradespeople needed to complete the project.

- ✓ *Benefit 1:* You haven't got to spend hours getting hold of quotes from lots of different people, and then hours organising them to turn up in the right sequence at the right time.
- ✓ *Benefit 2:* You can be sure that you've avoided the cowboys because it's my reputation that's at stake, so I only work with tried, tested and trusted craftspeople.
- ✓ *Benefit 3:* You can be sure that the project will turn out as it was designed, because I'll be making sure quality standards are met.

Summarising these benefits down, what Sara's clients are going to get is:

"A beautifully designed room that you can be confident you'll be delighted with, that fits its purpose perfectly, and feels great to spend time in. All this with minimum cost time, stress and worry."

This is the core message that Sara will want to ensure she gets across to her clients. It's a bit more enticing than her list of features, and as you'll realise as you work through the other steps of the programme, this will form the basis for a lot of her future communication.

Step 3. I can explain the benefits I offer clients succinctly and memorably to people I meet

Taking the principle that anyone within a one metre radius of you at any time is a potential client for your services, I'd encourage you to make sure you are able to take advantage of any opportunity that presents itself to let people know how you can help them.

To do this, you need to have a short audio logo that you feel confident saying and that people will register and remember. It's also a good answer to the question, "And what do you do?..." Having a well thought out quick reply that piques their interest to find out more will enable you to start a potentially interesting conversation.

Attraction in Action:

1. Write your audio logo to make it as memorable as possible – my favourite belongs to an architect I know, it's "I draw buildings". However, you may not be able to make yours quite as succinct as that and still get your message over successfully. The following formula is a useful starting point:
I .... help/work with/make… for/design… for/write… for – whatever is appropriate
PEOPLE .... label your target group, e.g. "busy professionals", "creative entrepreneurs", "retired couples"
WHO .... describe your client's desire or pain here, the reason they would want to spend their money with someone like you
SO THAT............... and here's where you insert the most appealing benefit from the list you made in step 2.

So mine might read: "I help creative entrepreneurs attract clients so they can spend more time doing what they love and less time doing marketing."

This works well when you've already got someone's attention, or the space in which to say this much.

2. The next step is to shorten it down to an attention grabbing headline, ideally of about 6 or 7 words, which prompts the question "How do you do that?" Here's what I might say, "I'm in the attraction business" or "I help people who are frustrated finding clients".

3. Test your various logos out on friends and colleagues and adjust them as necessary, until you're getting the response back that you want.

4. Learn your audio logo off by heart so you can sound really confident when you say it to total strangers.

5. Use it at every opportunity.

Going back to Sara, the interior designer, you'll remember that she'd decided that the main benefits she offered were, "A beautifully designed room that you can be confident you'll be delighted with, that fits its purpose perfectly, and feels great to spend time in. All this with minimum cost time, stress and worry."

So, combining her benefit list and the formula above, her logo might be:

"I work for busy people who want beautifully designed rooms that are delightful to see and live in."

Her shortened version might be, "I design beautiful rooms for busy people" or "I give you confidence in your interiors".

Don't worry about finding the perfect audio logo, just go with what feels right for now, and fine–tune it as necessary over time. After all, it's better to have something less than perfect that works than to simply mumble away vaguely about what you do until your contact's eyes glaze over!

Step 4. I know exactly which clients I can help the most and why

Often when people start in business they are happy to take on any work they can find. The thought of narrowing down their target client market can feel quite scary. People often think, "If I define tightly who I want to work with then I might be turning somebody else away."

To take this step involves you letting go of your fears that you might not be able to find any clients. It's about overcoming your fear of lack and being able to trust that the attraction marketing process works. Once you apply the 30 steps I'm sharing you'll know for certain that you'll be able to draw to you not just enough clients, but the right clients.

In this country alone there are more than 50 million people who could possibly want your services. That's certainly more than I can cope with and might be too many clients for you to cope with too! So if you really only need 10 or 200 or 2000 clients a year, spending time deciding who you'd like those clients to be will bring you the satisfaction in the future of working with only the people you really like. The people you can help best.

Attraction in Action:

1. Decide and write down how many clients you really want per year.

2. Think about the work you've done so far – which clients have you been able to help the most? Write down why those clients brought out the best work in you.

3. If you could choose to have a business full of these types of clients then what would they be like? Write down your answers.

I'll be totally honest here, and say I did struggle with this step for quite a few months when I first set up business. Remember, who did I want to coach? Anyone! I resisted hard when my coach asked me to narrow my target market down from anyone who wanted to be coached. She wasn't too impressed when I suggested adjusting it to 'anyone with some money who wanted to be coached' either.

Why did I resist? Partly because I really didn't know at the beginning who I wanted to work with, and I actually wanted to gain experience of a range of clients so I could choose where I was most effective. I wanted to keep my options open. But I also resisted due to a fear that by shutting the door on a particular area I might be missing out.

What I learned was:

1. FEAR stands for "Freezing Effective Action Response", and that the way to combat it is to do something – anything – but just do it.
2. One of my biggest fears was that I might pick the wrong area, and horror of horrors, get it wrong. I learned that it's perfectly okay to make a mistake, that's how we learn, by trying things, evaluating the results and trying something different.
3. Even when I chose a particular area to coach in, I still got enquiries from all sorts of other types of client as well.
4. And as you'll see, as my story progresses, once you start out on a track, all sorts of other influences start to align to guide you in the best direction. But I wasn't aware of them at that stage.

Step 5. I am aware of my unique selling point in my marketplace

Maybe you are the only person in the country supplying a particular product or service – if so, you can move straight on to the next question. If not, it's important to be able to define what is special about you that will make you stand out from the crowd.

For instance, we all have to buy some form of soap product to wash with, and yet the basis that we make our buying decision on is varied. Some of us decide by price, by the smell, by the packaging, will it match my bathroom. Others will want to know the soap is environmentally friendly or that it's kind to their skin. Obviously, one product cannot meet all of these criteria, and rather than try to be all things to all men, companies build their brands around just a few qualities. This gives them a focus for their marketing and makes them attractive to the people who care about those particular attributes.

If you were selling a product such as soap, the customer is buying that product. They can see it, smell it, and touch it. If however you are selling a service, what you are selling to your client or customer is less tangible. Part of the reason that the client decides to work with you rather than with someone else will be that they feel drawn to something within you as a person. This is especially important when they're putting their trust in you. They have to take you at your word that you can produce the results they are looking for. Clients will also pick up on a subtle level when you're not being yourself. They may not be able to put their finger on it but they'll know when you're not being authentic which can make them shy away from you. We are all more attracted to people who are comfortable in their own skin. People who are happy to be unique.

Attraction in Action:

Your aim is to identify what makes you different from all the other companies and professionals in your particular market – and you are unique. You can use some or all of the suggested activities below to help you with this:

1. How would you describe yourself if you were writing to someone you had never met?
2. Ask a trusted friend to tell you how they would describe you. What qualities do they think you have? And then ask a few more friends, and your family too, and watch out for the words that keep coming up.
3. Think back over your life and history, and note down the defining events, those that have made you who you are today, and the main interests you have had.
4. Make a list of the influences you feel are currently present in your life and work.
5. Think of other people in your profession and ask yourself "How am I different from person A, B, C?" and so on.
6. If you were a bar of soap, how would you be described? Another tough question, I'm afraid, but one that's worth taking time over. I decided that as a bar of soap I'd be: gentle yet effective, able to really clean deeply but leaving you feeling wonderfully soft. I'd probably be green. One of the coaches I worked with for a while would have definitely been a yellow coal tar soap, rather astringent, who could really strip away any dirt and leave you feeling scrubbed, a little sore but really fresh and new. What kind of soap are you?

Step 6. I add additional value to all my clients

Often what makes a real impression on us as customers is the little things. The things that don't cost much at all but tell us that they've thought about us and our needs.

I was very impressed recently when I returned an item to a shop called *Tchibo*, a coffee chain who sell a range of household and clothing items. I was offered a free cup of coffee because I'd had to bring something back. Now they had the coffee there anyway, the cost of which to them is negligible, but I'm now recommending them to you because I was impressed with the unexpected 'added value' they gave me.

In general, I'm far more likely to give referrals to a service provider who has gone the extra mile (even inch) for me than for someone who has simply met the terms of their contract. An acceptable level of service is expected, but an exceptional level of service gets remembered.

Adding unexpected additional value is also a way of making your service stand out from the crowd. It can form part of your unique selling point, which we looked at in Step 5.

Attraction in Action:

Your aim is to identify what added value you could give to your clients:

1. Make a list of all the elements that make up your service to your clients.
2. Examine each element and think what could you add for free, and at little cost, that would make an impression on your client.
3. It might help to imagine yourself as the client. What little extra would you like to receive. What would make the most difference to you?
4. Surprise your clients with your added value bonus, and again, monitor their reaction and be prepared to try a different one until you find what works for you and them.

Summary of Chapter Two

You should now be clear and able to answer yes to the following statements:

- ❑ I am in a position of 'visibility' to my ideal clients
- ❑ I am very clear about the benefits I offer my clients
- ❑ I can explain these benefits succinctly and memorably to people I meet
- ❑ I know exactly which clients I can help the most and why
- ❑ I am aware of my unique selling point in my marketplace
- ❑ I add additional value to all my clients.

Chapter Three – The Practical Work of Marketing

Marketing is about telling people what you do, again and again and again and again and...

This chapter shows you the steps you can take to build a sustainable marketing plan.

Step 7. I have a basic understanding of selling skills

I've always felt very uneasy with the idea of 'selling techniques' and very wary when I think I'm being 'sold to' by someone. Nobody likes to be manipulated and not many of us like to be a manipulator. I've also been on the receiving end of a lot of unwelcome telephone cold calls. I knew for a fact that I didn't want to spend my time and energy doing that.

So I avoided anything to do with selling like the plague. In fact, the first draft of this book had this step as simply, 'find out about selling skills'. This didn't cut any ice with my publishers so I've now researched the subject thoroughly. To my surprise and delight, I've found out that I've been selling to my prospective clients all along – I just thought I was having a conversation with them, finding out about them, and answering their queries. It turns out that a lot of selling is simply common sense, but like many things in life I just needed to have that pointed out to me.

Attraction in Action:

1. Read the article below, "How to sell your services".
2. Compare the selling process described below with what you do. Where are there similarities, and what do you do differently? What results are you getting?
3. Write down what you intend doing differently as a result of your comparisons.
4. Evaluate your results once you've tried out your new approaches.

How To "Sell" Your Services

Selling your services is one of those areas that's surrounded by myths that can make some people fear it. So let's demystify the process.

Firstly, what's the difference between 'marketing' and 'selling'? Marketing is the process of identifying and communicating with people that are prospective clients; selling is the process of persuading a particular prospective client to buy from you.

The aim of good marketing, and particularly of the attraction marketing process, is for the selling part of the process to become unnecessary, because the client has already decided they want to work with you before they have even contacted you. Nonetheless, knowing that every interaction with someone brings you either closer or further away from them, having an understanding of the theory of selling is still useful.

The sales process is made up of six steps, which are:

1. planning and/or preparation
2. introduction or opening
3. questioning
4. presentation
5. overcoming objections/negotiating
6. closing the sale

Let's look at each of those steps in more detail:

1. Planning and/or preparation

The obvious steps are to ensure that any literature you use, any samples, or a portfolio of previous work, are as you want them. Less obvious steps are:

- ✓ Think about what your prospective clients requirements are likely to be, based on the information you've gleaned in setting up the appointment.
- ✓ Make sure you're really clear on what the benefits are of what you offer.
- ✓ Really know what you want to get over to your prospect, and the ideal order in which to do this. Rehearse this until it feels totally comfortable.
- ✓ Think carefully about what you want from the meeting, and spend some time visualising a positive outcome.
- ✓ Approach the meeting with the attitude, 'If they want to buy, that's great, and if they don't, well that's ok too'. This stops you coming over as needy or pushy.
- ✓ Plan your personal image – what do the clothes you wear and your overall appearance say about you?

2. Introduction or opening

People form opinions of you based on information gained in the first few moments of meeting you, so creating a good first impression and setting the scene is vital for the success of the meeting.

- ✓ Remember to smile when introducing yourself.
- ✓ Your aim is to develop a rapport with your prospect – however it's important to move on to what you came for promptly rather than chatting the meeting away.
- ✓ Ask how much time your client has available and agree a time to finish.
- ✓ Check whether your client would prefer you to give him your presentation first or for you to ask him questions.

3. Questioning

From a selling perspective, the purpose of questioning, as well as for you to understand what your client wants, is for you to become clear about which benefits of your services are going to matter most to your client. This enables you to stress those benefits in your presentation. These normally relate to an emotion of some kind, as people buy with their emotions and then justify their purchases afterwards with logic.

- ✓ The client should be talking and you listening/writing notes at this point. Don't get drawn in to explaining how what you can do meets his requirements until you're totally clear on what he wants.
- ✓ People love being listened to well, which builds the rapport between you and the client.
- ✓ When dealing with a couple or a group of people, the questioning process also allows you to work out who the decision

maker is. You can then match the benefits you offer to those preferred by the decision maker.

- ✓ The questioning process allows you to find out whether your client is serious about the project, and also whether they have the necessary budget. There may seem little point carrying on with your full presentation if it's become obvious that your expectations are worlds apart.
- ✓ It also allows you to check out whether this client is someone you wish to work for or not – you're interviewing them just as much as they're assessing you.

4. Presentation

Your presentation now needs to show the client how you can meet their needs.

- ✓ Use your presentation to help the client imagine how they will feel when you've completed the work for them. Let your words light up their imagination, so that they can really sense what the finished result will give them.
- ✓ Many sales are lost because the person selling doesn't recognise when the client's ready to buy, and just keeps on going. As the saying goes, "once you've sold, shut up!"
- ✓ Drop information from your presentation on points that are not of interest to your client – you'll know which these are from the questioning process.
- ✓ Make sure the language you use is suited to your audience, and don't get overly technical or use jargon. Nobody likes a "know–it–all" so don't do anything that will make your prospect less likely to use your services.
- ✓ You'll undermine your own presentation and credibility if you're rude about your competition in any way.

5. Overcoming objections

Many people hear an objection as a "No" and back off defeated. But an objection is little more than feedback telling you the prospective client is considering what you're saying. It's often just a request for further information and clarity.

- ✓ If you hear an objection, resist the temptation to repeat part of your presentation again or to explain why that shouldn't be an issue – as it certainly is for your client.
- ✓ If you hear an objection, use it as an opportunity to ask your prospect to tell you more about the issue and why it's important to him. Once you've got the full picture, you can then negotiate with the client to find an acceptable solution.
- ✓ Welcome objections – once you've handled all of them, step 6, closing the sale becomes almost redundant!

6. Closing the sale

If you've followed steps 1–5, all you need to do here is to say, "Are you happy that we've covered everything and would you like to go ahead?" That's it. No clever closes, pitches or manipulations. Just a straightforward question that requires an answer.

- ✓ This gives the prospect the chance to check they have covered all their objections.
- ✓ It makes it easy for the client to say yes – if you don't say it, they can sometimes feel uncomfortable about what to do next. Once they've said yes, let them know what will happen next – e.g. "I'll have the concept drawings ready for you in two weeks, can we make an appointment now for you to see them", "I'll get the contract in the post to you tomorrow to sign." etc. Saying yes is usually the most difficult part of the whole conversation for the

customer, so anything you can do to make it easier will help them to go ahead as they want.

✓ If they say, "I'll think about it", you'll need to treat this as another objection and find out what's behind it – it maybe that they just feel uncomfortable saying no, or it maybe that they're genuinely cautious and want to mull things over before proceeding. You'll then need to agree what the next action is, e.g. "I'll phone you on Wednesday to hear what you've decided".

✓ If they say, "no thanks", at this point then at least you can focus your attention on more suitable prospects.

So, I hope that this has helped debunk any beliefs you might have had about 'I can't sell my services' and that you've realised, as I did, that the sales process in itself is a straightforward one. Approach each of the steps with confidence, and enjoy the results!

Step 8. I have a clear picture/description of my ideal client

If you completed Step 4, this step will be easy for you. In Step 4, you identified how many clients you wanted annually and which clients you felt you were most able to help, and thus were most likely to benefit from your services.

This step asks you to look more closely at the target group of clients you have identified, and to select just one person as the absolutely "perfect client", the one that if your business consisted solely of working with people like them, you would be overjoyed. You may have to create a composite picture, built on characteristics and qualities from various clients, and that's fine.

Once you know who your perfect client is, you can then target your communication to appeal just to them, thus saving you vast amounts of wasted time, money and energy trying to attract the wrong people.

If you're clear about who you work best with, it makes it easier for people to pinpoint potential referrals for you as you've narrowed down the search group for them. It's the difference between asking someone "Do you know anyone who might be interested in having a special sports massage?" and asking, "Do you know any women who play squash? I've got this new knee treatment that can help them."

The first question is too vague while the second helps us remember likely people far more easily. In this example, you could also target your marketing more effectively, by making contact with the local sports clubs and offering them your services – this would probably net you a better uptake on your services than putting an ad in your local paper.

Attraction in Action:

Your aim is to have a clear picture or description of your ideal client and their lifestyle. Think about your clients/customers to date. Which of them has been the client you enjoyed working with the most?

1. Write a list of the qualities and characteristics you valued in them. If there were things about them you didn't like, turn them round into the positive opposite – for example, if one client was great except that they always delayed paying you, which irritated you, you know that 'pays me promptly' needs to be on your list for the perfect client.
2. Now think about the rest of your clients/customers and repeat the process, until you have a full description of your ideal client.
3. Think about this person and write down your answers to these questions so you can build up a clear image of him/her:
   - What are their needs and concerns?
   - Which of the benefits on your list from Step 2 will appeal to them most?
   - What is their lifestyle like? Where do they live, what do they read, how do they spend their money and their leisure time?
   - What influences them to spend their money?
   - What else can you identify about them?

I do regret that I delayed doing this exercise. Just after I'd decided to work full time as a coach, after a year of working part time while I was training, I inadvertently stumbled on parts of the attraction marketing system, and started using it, and getting results. I had decided that what I really wanted was to be hired by one new client per week, as that would be manageable. And so for 26 weeks, barring Christmas, I didn't want any new clients then, I was hired by a new client each week.

Unfortunately I was using the attraction marketing system without really understanding how it worked. I was getting hired alright, and some of my clients were wonderful to work with – but many of them weren't. A few didn't want to pay, one didn't want to face up to the issues we uncovered in the first session and never came back, another insisted on face to face meetings in a crowded pub, and so on. These examples were all reflecting areas of my business practice that I needed to look at and set some firm policies and boundaries on. I did learn from each experience, but looking back, oh how I wish I had defined my Ideal Client much earlier on.

Here's the list of my Ideal Client's Qualities that I made from looking back on those clients gained, and in many cases, lost again in that six month period:

- ✓ Takes responsibility for their own progress
- ✓ Prepared to take big steps
- ✓ Decisive
- ✓ Interested in the attraction process
- ✓ Open–minded
- ✓ Intuitive
- ✓ Aware of their spirituality
- ✓ Open & honest
- ✓ Willing to trust me
- ✓ Wants a long term partnership
- ✓ Brings a range of issues
- ✓ Prefers telephone coaching
- ✓ Tells her contacts about me

- ✓ Interested in self development
- ✓ Wants to grow and move forward
- ✓ Willing to listen, have a 'coaching' conversation
- ✓ Committed to the process
- ✓ Does the homework
- ✓ Reliable, keeps appointments
- ✓ Pays my full fee willingly
- ✓ Earns or has access to money
- ✓ Does not need counselling

The practical advantage to me is that now when I'm talking with a potential client, I'm assessing them against my shopping list of qualities, just as much as they're checking out whether they want to work with me. And because I now understand so much better how the attraction marketing system works, I only get contacted by clients who meet the above criteria.

Step 9. I know what I want my business to be like in 1, 3 & 5 years time

So far you've worked out what the service is that you offer, who benefits from it most and who you really want to offer it to. This step is about creating the master plan for your business, your map, so you can chart the route you'll have to take to reach your destination. And if you don't have a clue about where that destination is, how do you know which direction to take next?

This is your Business Plan. It is not cast in stone, it is a working document that you can add to and alter as your business progresses and evolves. It is however essential that you create one, even if you're only willing at this stage to create it one year in advance. For many people who are not sure where they want to go, looking five years into the future seems daunting or just plain silly. On the other hand, maybe you'd like to expand your plan to where you'd like yourself to be in 10 or 20 years time.

An important factor to remember is that you will also be evolving as the life of your business goes by, and that what you consider yourself capable of now, or maybe next year has the potential to stretch enormously by the time you've reached year 3 or 5 or 10. So I'd encourage you to dream a little here as you do this Business Plan, and to imagine that anything is possible for you.

Attraction in Action:

1. The aim is to write your Business Plan:
2. Decide over what span you want to write the plan, 1, 3 or 5 years.
3. Using the layout template below, write your plan. I've included the plan that I wrote in 2002 as an example.
   a) Mission Statement – what is the overall aim of your business, and what is the core purpose of your business?
   b) Business Goals – what do you want to have achieved by that time? This needs to be expressed in solid facts and figures. What do you want to be earning and what turnover and profit will you need to make to do that? How many clients do you want to be working with per week or per year?
   c) Operations & Management – where will you be working from? How many hours a week do you want to work? Will you employ staff? How many?
   d) Sales & Marketing –The greatest needs of my target customers which I aim to fulfil – you'll have already identified this from steps 2 & 8, Your Benefits & Identifying Your Ideal Client.
   e) I am different to my competition – your unique selling point from step 5.
   f) I will market to this client group via these methods – leave this part blank for now, and we'll add to it after the next step, step 10.
   g) Finances – how much money will be coming in (and from where) and going out (to where)?

Here's the plan I wrote in 2002 to cover the year 2003. It's very simple, but who said choosing a destination and planning the route had to be complicated?

Trellis Coaching Business Plan for 2003

Mission Statement: My aim is to encourage and support the personal and business growth of my clients – successful business owners and professionals who are serious enough about their success to be willing to invest in themselves and to take risks and actions to achieve it. I offer telephone and face–to–face coaching which is focused around the Laws of Attraction.

Business Goals:

1. To build a full practice of 40 clients who have one or more 45 min coaching session per 3 week month, via phone or face–to–face. I also offer 2 low–fee coaching places.
2. To have arrangements with a number of associate coaches to coach other clients.
3. To develop a number of passive revenue streams.

Operations & Management: I run Trellis Coaching from my home with the help of a PA (4hrs per a week), and a VA (as required). I bring in the services of associate coaches as required.

I work 4 days per week, except during school holidays when I work 2 days per week. I work with clients for 3 weeks, and the fourth week is used for developing new services, meetings, marketing and other activities important to the growth of the business.

Sales & Marketing:

The greatest needs of my target customers that I aim to help them with:

1. Finding a consistent flow of suitable clients
2. Feeling overwhelmed and stressed by the pressures of business
3. Lack of a clear direction and focus
4. Feeling frustrated with the inability to meet their goals.

I am different to my competition:

1. I offer a choice of 1 or 2 sessions per month, allowing more flexibility
2. I expect to work with my clients for many years as part of their support systems.
3. I offer coaching based around the Laws of Attraction
4. I am uniquely me!

I will market to this client group via:

1. Networking groups
2. Newsletters
3. Website

Finances: As of December 02, the practice has 20 clients paying fees ranging between £40 and £95 per hour. It is planned that 2 new clients will be introduced each month throughout 2003 at a fee of £95 per 45 min session, bringing the total number of clients to approximately 40. Fees for existing clients will gradually be brought in line with this rate. By the beginning of 2004, monthly fee income will be £3800."

Some of this plan worked out exactly, and some parts didn't, because they evolved into better things, as I discovered more about attraction marketing.

Step 10. I have a written marketing plan

There is something about writing ideas down and turning them into a 'plan' that makes them more concrete for you, it helps you feel clear on what you're going to be doing, and can remove the dithering of "well I could try this or maybe that or..." It also enables you to be realistic about how much time you have and to set yourself goals to aim for.

This step involves you drawing together all the factors that you've identified to date and creating from them a working marketing plan. From this you will know where you are going to be spending your time, effort and money on making yourself visible to your ideal clients.

Attraction in Action:

Your aim is to create an overall marketing plan, with several different campaigns, rather than a series of unconnected bouts of marketing activity.

1. Look at each of the ideas on your step 1 list, the list of all the possible ways of meeting future clients, and consider them from the perspective of those ideal clients you want to meet, and what you know of them. Make a list of your possible marketing activities. If you've decided that advertising is the way to go for you, which publications does your ideal client read? If you like talking to people, where can you go to meet your ideal clients?
2. Then run these ideas through the filter of:
    a) How many clients do you actually want? If you only need 5 per year, an exhibition stand at a show visited by 100,000 people might bring you too many enquiries to handle. Be realistic about your outcomes.

b) How much time can you devote to marketing? Decide what percentage of your business's total working hours you wish to give over to marketing, whether you employ staff to do your marketing or undertake it all yourself. This figure can be reviewed and altered as you monitor the results of your marketing, and also allows you to work out a realistic fee structure that ensures your non–fee earning hours are 'paid for' by your fee earning hours. Remember you're planning an ongoing campaign, one that can be sustained over the long term rather than one that brings you an influx of clients followed by a dearth of them when you decide to stop marketing.

c) How much money do you want to spend?

3. Play the Fan Base Game:
   - Choose 10 people that you know.
   - Place them as appropriate in one of the boxes on the sheet below.
   - With each person, work out a strategy to move them one box across the sheet – i.e. what do you need to do to move them from being someone that 'you know' to someone who 'knows you're a garden designer?' What can you do to move another contact from someone who 'knows you're a designer' to someone who 'knows you're actively looking for clients' and would appreciate any help they could give you?

– Once you've moved everyone one box to the right, what do you need to do to move them onto the next box?

The aim of the game is to get all 10 moved into your totally committed Fan box. Then start, if necessary, with another list of 10 names, and design strategies to convert them, step by step, into people who will give you regular referrals.

4. You'll now have an adjusted list of activities for consideration for inclusion in your marketing plan. Now select up to three of the activities to work on for increasing your visibility. Working on more than three areas at one time dissipates your energies too much, you can always come back to other activities on your list at a later point so just pick 3 for now.
5. For each activity, write down your goal, and then break it down into the steps that you will need to take to reach that goal.
6. Take the first action step towards each of the goals.
7. Congratulate yourself then move on to the second step. And so on...

Template For The Fan Base Game

	Someone I know	Someone who knows what I do	Someone who knows I'm looking for clients	Someone who has referred me	A Fan! someon[e] who regularly refers me
1.					
2.					
3.					
4.					
5.					
6.					
7.					
8					
9					
10.					

Let's use Selina, the glamorous mobile beauty therapist, as an example. Her "Being Comfortably Visible" list included:

- ✓ Delivering leaflets about her service
- ✓ Sign writing her car
- ✓ Advertising in the local paper
- ✓ Holding a nail party for her friends

Her ideal client was:

- ✓ Female
- ✓ Young 20–35
- ✓ Cares about her appearance and likes to look cool
- ✓ Can afford to have her nails done regularly
- ✓ Employed
- ✓ Friendly
- ✓ Tells her friends about my service
- ✓ Goes out socialising a lot
- ✓ Fun loving
- ✓ Want her nails done in the evenings

So let's take a look at Selina's list of activities for becoming more visible list from her ideal client's perspective:

1. Delivering leaflets. Selina's already tried this without much success by leaving leaflets in pubs and cafes. Her ideal client is probably too busy having fun in the pub to notice a leaflet – perhaps the hairdressers might be a better place for these?

2. Sign writing her car. Her ideal client might notice this, but would they be likely to write the number down? How many people would see the car who weren't her ideal clients?

3. Advertising in the local paper. How often do young fun loving women sit down and read their local paper? Selina could be advertising to many thousands of people who aren't her ideal clients.

4. Holding a nail party for her friends. Her ideal clients might well enjoy a fun evening out with the girls, and they may well be attracted to using Selina again because they want some of her glamour to rub off on them.

The next step is to run it through the time/money/number of clients filter, and adjust these ideas further. Selina wants to work with just 10 clients per week until she builds her confidence and her client base, and gives up her full time job. She therefore has a very limited time for marketing, perhaps 2 evenings a week initially, dropping to one as her client base builds.

Bearing these facts in mind, she decides to develop the nail party idea, distributing vouchers to attendees to give to their friends for a future half price treatment or free treatment if they host another nail evening.

I appreciate that Selina's business is only small at this stage, and yet her example shows how a considered approach to all the factors enables you to produce a successful marketing plan that ties in with your business goals, your resources and what you find comfortable to do.

Step 11. I set goals and targets for my business and marketing and review them regularly

You now have your Business Plan created, which sets your long–term goal, and also forms the starting point for deciding on your shorter term goals. You also have your Marketing Plan.

Having a goal in place stretches you to achieve more than you might without it and helps you formulate your action plans. Set your goals high, even though you don't know at the moment how you can possibly achieve them. If you allow yourself to settle for smaller goals, because they seem more manageable now, you'll never surprise yourself with what has become possible for you. People have a tendency to achieve just under the goal they've set themselves, so setting the bar for your goals higher than you think possible means that you'll end up achieving even more than you ever thought you could – as it says in the quote by an unknown author "Aim for the stars, and you might reach the sky".

Attraction in Action:

1. Look at your Business Plan and break it down into a series of shorter term goals. If you know what you want in three years time, what needs to be in place in 18 months time for that to happen? Write it down.
2. And for your 18 month plan to come about, what needs to have come about within 9 months? Write that down.
3. And for your 9 month plan to materialise, what needs to materialise within 4 months? Write it down.
4. For your 4 month plan to happen, what needs to be happen within 2 months? Write it down.
5. Carry on, looking next at what needs to be place in 1 month's time. Write it down.
6. Finally, decide what you can do this week to bring your 3 year vision into being, and do it!

I regularly use the above process and find it works really well in making my Business Plan manageable. I've broken the big picture down into manageable pieces and because I'm always clear on what the next step needs to be I'm confident that things are heading in the right direction.

Having goals can support you in achieving amazing results – for example, I remember writing down what seemed like a huge number of newsletter subscribers I wanted in three years time. The number I needed for the next month was quite manageable and the next and the next. Before I knew it I'd ended up, with seemingly little effort, achieving my three–year target six months early.

Step 12. I monitor results regularly and adjust my marketing plan accordingly

One definition of lunacy is to keep on doing what you're doing and expecting different results. If you want to keep your marketing effort to a minimum then you need to capitalise on the activities that bring you the best results – I know it sounds obvious, but many people don't monitor the effectiveness of their marketing so have no idea what works and what doesn't.

Attraction in Action:

1. For each of your chosen steps for increasing visibility, decide how long you're willing to try them out before selecting another one to try. Of course, many activities don't bring you instant success, but you don't want to carry on using one method indefinitely if it's not working effectively for you – set a time limit.
2. Devise a system for monitoring your results. This might be as simple as always asking enquirers where they got your details from, and logging their answer somewhere suitable.
3. Set a future date in your diary to do a cost/reward comparison for each activity – if your networking group is costing you £1000 per year but is bringing you £10k's worth of business, that's obviously a better investment than the £50 advert that doesn't bring you anything. The vital part is to do the sums.
4. Schedule a regular time each week or month to look at your results and your marketing plan and modify it if necessary.

Now is probably a good point to consider using 'networking' as a marketing tool. My experience, when I was running the ladies supper group, was that quite a few of the ladies who were new in business would come along to a meeting or maybe two, and then say, "I didn't get any work from it, so there's no point going along to any more." Their mindset was that of the hunter, they were looking for what they could get out of it in the short term. But as any experienced networker knows selling to everyone you meet is not what networking is about.

The principle of 'givers gain' lies at the heart of networking. The rules are quite simple, "If I give you business, you will want to give me business", and it is also a vital part of the attraction principle to first give out what you're hoping to attract. In fact, 'givers gain' is not quite right, it's giving without the motivation of immediate gain that seems to bring back double, even treble the value to us.

Networking is about building up relationships with people, getting to know them, connecting them with other people who could help them. It's having the mindset of being a farmer and cultivating your connections, rather than that of the hunter, in for a quick killing and then away again. The hunter has to keep searching for new prey, whereas the farmer reaps benefits from all the seeds sown in the early days. And if he saves some seed and replants it, feeds and waters it, he'll then have another crop to harvest the next season. I'm still getting, and giving, regular referrals from the contacts I made through the supper group several years after it folded. Plus there's a lot to be said for the personal friendships you can develop.

Step 13. I allocate regular planning time to my marketing

This builds on the previous step, and asks that you agree to spend regular time planning your marketing as a part of a review of your whole business strategy. This review is akin to the Board Meetings that all large companies hold regularly, and small companies often don't, because they're too busy. These meetings give the directors an opportunity to reflect on the overall direction of their company and to agree on the main thrust of their activities. The overall direction is often more important than concentrating on the finer detail. It's an opportunity to review your Business Plan and to adjust the Marketing Plan to ensure you're on track.

Attraction in Action:

1. Decide how frequently you would like to do a review. I find a monthly "Board Meeting" works for me but your timescale might be different.
2. Block out a time in your diary to hold your own "Board Meeting", and ensure that you keep this date with yourself. Remember that successful entrepreneurs are those who allocate time to working 'on' their business, rather than just working 'in' it.
3. Think about how some outside support would help you stick to the schedule of "Board Meetings" you've decided on, rather than you abandoning the meeting because of some other interruption. Would your meeting be more productive if you had a Chairman of some kind, who ensured you stayed on track and on time? Step 19 talks more about the benefits of outside support for the solo business.

Step 14. I take consistent, persistent action on my marketing to avoid the yo–yo effect

The classic marketing pattern for small businesses is that they treat marketing like a yo–yo activity. This means that they initially undertake a splurge of marketing which brings them some clients (and probably not ideal ones). At this point they stop marketing as they're too busy doing the work for these clients. For some businesses where each client becomes a long term customer, this may be sufficient to establish a satisfactory client base, but for many businesses who need a continual stream of new business, the result is that, once they've finished the work for their original clients, they discover they have no new work, so have to start right back at the beginning again. To avoid this feast or famine scenario, marketing needs to form part of your weekly business activity, even when you're busy with clients.

In fact, for your marketing to consistently bring you the results you want, you need to make it a habitual thing that you do regardless how busy you are or of what else is going on. Marketing should be somewhat akin to brushing your teeth twice a day.

If you can create a MAD habit – "Marketing Actions Daily" – you'll achieve far more over the long term. Let me illustrate this with an example; imagine you've decided that an important part of your marketing is making follow up phone calls to potential clients, and you've allocated Friday afternoons to do this. You make your list of, say, 25 people to call and start ringing round, only to find that half of them are out, or have gone home early – it's very easy to feel demoralised at this point, and you've then got to wait until the following Friday to ring them back again.

How much better would it be to build making a certain number of follow up calls into a MAD habit, and ensure that you make your five calls first thing every morning? If you have to phone back, you can phone back the next day, rather than a week later, and once you've made your calls you can then get on with the rest of your work knowing that you've done your marketing for the day!

Attraction in Action:

1. Look again at your marketing plan – does it include activities each week that will move you closer to gaining ideal clients? If not, what could you introduce that would help your marketing effort be sustainable over the long term?
2. Decide if any of your marketing activities could be broken down to form the basis of a MAD habit – "Marketing Actions Daily".
3. What can you do to build the habit up? For example, you could decide to reward yourself in some way once you've managed five consecutive days of the MAD habit, or maybe revert to your childhood and make yourself a star chart. Whatever it takes to make marketing as much an established part of your daily routines as brushing your teeth – do it!

Summary of Chapter Three

You've now done the practical work of designing and starting to implement a sustainable marketing plan. So you should be able to answer yes to the following...

- ❑ I have a basic understanding of selling skills
- ❑ I can identify my ideal client and have a clear picture/description of them
- ❑ I know what I want my business to be like in 1, 3 & 5 years time
- ❑ I have a written marketing plan
- ❑ I set goals and targets for my business and marketing and review them regularly
- ❑ I monitor results regularly and adjust my marketing plan accordingly
- ❑ I allocate regular planning time to my marketing
- ❑ I take consistent, persistent action on my marketing, to avoid the yo–yo effect

Chapter Four – The Attraction Work

To date you've been developing all the ingredients that will go to make up your attraction mix. You've become very clear on who you are, what you offer and who you're offering it to and you've laid the foundations of a successful marketing habit by developing your marketing muscles and MAD habits.

Now you're going to learn about a special law that adds the magic to your attraction mix. A law that allows you to attract all the ideal clients you want.

This special law is one that is around us all the time, the effects of which we all experience every day. Becoming aware of this law and how it operates will enable you to work in alignment with it to your advantage. Enter, "The Universal Laws of Attraction!"

It's all about Energy

Have you noticed how some people seem to be born lucky? Opportunities seem to just turn up out of the blue for them. They have a habit of being in the right place at the right time, and on the whole life appears to be relatively effortless. You could say they lived a charmed existence. And yet for other people, life seems to be a struggle, where one disaster after another befalls them.

In your own life, can you remember times when you've wanted something to happen, or you've set out to achieve something, or to acquire something, and it has all worked out really effortlessly, as if it was just meant to be. Yet at other times, you've had to strive and struggle. You were beset with obstacles at every turn? What do you put this down to? Is it divine will, or fate, or a random lucky or unlucky circumstance or 'just one of those things'?

In his recent book entitled, "How to Be Lucky", psychologist Dr Richard Wiseman carried out scientifically sound statistical surveys on people who considered themselves to be successful and lucky. What he discovered was that these people shared certain characteristics:

- ✓ They had an optimistic outlook on life.
- ✓ They had an expectation that life would work out well.

- ✓ They often followed their intuitive hunches.
- ✓ And they were able to look for the gift in difficult situations.

There is another explanation being put forward, which recent developments in quantum physics are moving towards being able to prove, but which many people's anecdotal evidence and experiences support. This theory builds on Dr Wiseman's observations regarding lucky people. It states that there exist Universal Laws of Attraction that hold good for how the world operates just as the Laws of Gravity determine what happens when your toast slips off your plate.

According to these laws, we attract to us what we focus on, so that the lucky people who expect things to work out well find that they do. Likewise, those people who think life's just one bad thing after another, discover they've attracted to them yet another bad thing. You could say that in this way we really do create our own reality.

How does this work? I am not a physicist so can only give you a simple explanation of the theory; what I do have is personal experience of the law working for me. I also can't explain the Law of Gravity to you in any great depth, but I know how I experience that working too.

The theory behind the Laws of Attraction is all down to energy. When I was at school studying chemistry, I was told that all objects were made up of molecules, and inside the molecules were atoms. I didn't even consider neutrons, electrons and protons which are inside the atoms either, but at that time scientists believed that these were the smallest bits of matter that formed the building blocks of everything in our universe.

Then quarks were discovered, which were even smaller bits of matter. So quarks were then thought to be the smallest. Then along came string theory, which is still being hotly debated by scientists today. String theory maintains that the basic building blocks of life are minute strings of pure energy, which vibrate at certain frequencies to take certain forms. According to string theory experts, the strings of energy inside a table are vibrating at the frequency that means they manifest, to our eyes, as a wooden table. The strings of energy inside the atoms of the molecules of the carpet the table is sitting on are vibrating at a different frequency, which we experience as a woolly carpet. And the strings of energy within us vibrate at frequencies that show up in this world as a human being. If you'd like to read more about the science behind the theory in an accessible way, I recommend you read 'The Field: The Quest for The Secret Force in the Universe' by Lynne McTaggart.

Because we are living things as opposed to a static form such as a carpet or table, our energy levels can and do rise and fall. They alter not only on a physical level, dependent on how much food and rest and exercise we've had, but are also altered by how we feel. Our emotions affect our overall energy levels. The language we use supports this – we say things like, "he was in really high spirits yesterday", "I was feeling a bit down", "She was a bit low".

How does this affect us as business people? From a purely physical point of view, if you're feeling low and despondent about your prospects for success, you're less likely to feel like making your marketing calls. Whereas, if you're feeling great about what you offer, you'll find it easy to share your enthusiasm with your potential clients. But how you feel, how high or low your energy is, matters on another level too, and that's because of how the Laws of Attraction operate.

The Laws of Attraction

These Laws state that what you focus on is what you get. This is in fact the result of the way they operate, rather than the mechanics of how they operate. Remember the vibrating energy strings? According to the Laws of Attraction, energies that are vibrating at a particular frequency draw to them energies that are vibrating at a similar level. In her book 'Excuse Me, Your Life Is Waiting', Lyn Grabhorn talks about the analogy of a room full of thousands of tuning forks to illustrate the concept. She says that if you ping your tuning fork, the only ones in the room that will start pinging too are those that are tuned to the same frequency.

If you take the example of making your marketing calls, when you're feeling great your energy is vibrating at a higher frequency, and thus when you call people, you'll attract back to you energies vibrating at a similarly high level. But when your energy is low, you'll attract people with similarly low energies.

The Laws of Attraction are in operation all around us and most people are not aware of them operating. Because we're not aware, we don't work to raise our energies and attract better things to us. We tend to sometimes feel good, and sometimes not so good, so what we tend to attract to us is a range of circumstances that reflect our feelings – some good and some bad. The people who are naturally optimistic and positive are vibrating with higher energies than those that are naturally pessimistic and negative, and so the experiences they attract to themselves match their general expectations of life. So what you focus on is indeed what you get.

The way in which you work with the Laws of Attraction to create the reality you desire is firstly to have a crystal clear vision of what it is you wish to create. Then you need a method of magnetising that vision towards you – the fuel that you use to drive this manifestation process is emotion (emotion = E (energy) + motion). The laws of attraction state that what we focus on is what we get, and that like attracts like. So it follows that the higher the level of positive emotion that you are feeling, the more of the same positive feelings you will attract.

Now all of this may sound pretty farfetched but just because you can't see an atom it doesn't mean an atom doesn't exist. I now totally accept that these laws are operating because I've tested them for myself. By choosing to work with them I can achieve what I really want. So if you're sceptical right now, I challenge you to put what I'm saying to the test by trying it with an attitude of acceptance. I was sceptical too, but this change from a place of total scepticism to one of belief to the point where I'm delighted to be able to share what I've learned with you has come about purely through direct experience.

So, let's get started. Let's take the attraction steps that will enable you to create the reality of your successful business! I'll look at each of them from both the Attraction and the Physical viewpoint, so that you can still be gaining benefit from taking the actions, regardless whether you believe in the Laws of Attraction yet.

Step 15. I know how I will feel about my business in 1, 3 and 5 years time

This step sounds similar to Step 9, where you created your Business Plan, and it is, with one important difference. This step talks about how you will feel when you've achieved your plan.

This step involves shifting your dry old plan on a piece of paper, probably filed away and dragged out once a month for revision at your Board Meeting to a working, living document that inspires you everyday to take positive action on it. Rather than just a Business Plan, it becomes your vision of your future life.

Attraction in Action:

1. Read your Business Plan and imagine how you will feel when it is real for you. Then rewrite it as your personal vision by including those feelings too. Write it in the present tense, as if you already have what you would like in the future. Don't worry if you don't think you're particularly emotionally literate, there are only two types of feeling you need to think about – does what you imagine make you feel better than you are now (which is great) or worse (in which case you'd be advised to change what you're imagining).
2. Add into your written vision the description of your ideal client from step 8.
3. Sit and reread each part of the vision and imagine it until you physically feel that positive feeling. For example, as I read the part of my vision that talks about how delighted and excited I am by the success of the Attraction Marketing workshops, I feel a buzz of excitement in my stomach. I'll call this sensation the 'feeling place' of my vision.
4. When you're in the 'feeling place' of each section of your vision, choose an image or a sound or a smell that encapsulates

what you're visualising. For example you might choose to imagine a paying in sheet with a nice high figure on it, or to hear cries of "Well Done", or to smell the champagne as you celebrate a huge order. This will then act as a trigger, which enables you to reach the 'feeling place' again much more quickly than starting from scratch each time.

5. For the best effect, revisit your vision regularly, daily if possible, and spend a few minutes reaching the 'feeling place' of your future success.
6. Start keeping a Success Log in which you write down and celebrate those parts of the vision that are starting to materialise for you now.

You may think it strange to be asked to do visualisation work, and I can assure you that I did too. I didn't start doing this visualising until I'd already begun to lose my scepticism about the Laws of Attraction through other experiences. Doing this type of work was not new to me, but again I couldn't see the point of spending the time doing it if there wasn't going to be an immediate visible payback for it.

In fact, from a physical viewpoint, there is a payback. Imagine sitting down to a deliciously fragrant curry or steak and chips or whatever your favourite food is. As you imagine the plate in front of you, and you can see the food in your mind's eye, you can smell the wonderful aromas and taste the flavours, your mouth starts to salivate. Your body has prepared itself to eat this food based purely on your thoughts. Your unconscious mind has been fooled by your thinking. You can "act as if" something you had only imagined was real and your physiology will change also. In the same way, you can imagine your future business success as if you were experiencing it today, and your subconscious mind will act to support you.

From an Attraction perspective, as you imagine yourself being successful, so your vibration rises to match that of a successful person, and events and people are drawn towards you who match that vibration and help bring about your success.

Wanting something, and wanting it a lot, is the key. Again, if you really want something, and you're prepared to take action towards getting it, you'll be determined enough to overcome all obstacles and get what you want.

Have you ever wanted something and just known that somehow it was going to happen. Even if you had no idea how you just knew it would? I've had that experience a few times in my life, where it seems almost as if the Universe conspires to help you get what you really want. People ring up out of the blue, or an opportunity comes up in an unexpected way that brings you what you want effortlessly.

Effortlessness doesn't mean that you don't have to take any action, quite the contrary. There are many people who really want certain things in their lives but have a hundred and one reasons why they can't possibly do anything about it. Their wanting is never going to be more than a huge, puffed up, wish. You do have to take action to get what you want, but the sense of effortlessness comes because the process feels smooth and easy. Obstacles seem to fade away, the right people show up at the right time, and there's a sense of 'this was just meant to be'.

I didn't always believe success should be effortless, I needed proof that the process worked. If you remember back to step 8, defining my ideal client, I was doing something right, because I was really wanting a new client every week and I was taking action that made me visible, so the clients could find me. But what I wasn't doing was being clear about exactly who it was that I wanted, so I was getting an assorted mix of clients, and I didn't understand at that stage how my energy levels affected my results.

One of the experiments I tried once I did know more about raised vibrations and attraction was to ask for a referral that I could give at my breakfast networking meeting each week. By asking I mean just saying to myself, 'I want a referral for the meeting next week'. You have to ask before you can receive.

There was an expectation at the networking meeting that a referral be passed each week, and after the first few months of using the professional services of various members of the group for a variety of reasons I'd been meaning to get round to for ages, I was running short of referrals. So I started 'asking' for one each week, and trusting that one would show up in some form or another – and it did, without fail. I've carried on doing this for over a year now allowing me to pass on nearly fifty referrals to members at my breakfast meeting from third parties. After the first week, where my approach was, 'Well, I'll give this a try – I wonder if it'll work?' and it did, I thought it was just a happy chance. The second week I thought, 'I wonder if this will work again? Maybe it will and maybe it won't' – and it did! As the weeks went by, I became persuaded that this was happening too regularly for it to be coincidence. Something else was afoot. Even on the weeks where no referral had appeared before I went to the meeting, someone at the meeting would ask if anyone knew a hypnotherapist or a book publisher, and lo and behold, I would. I began to reach a point where I could move from a place of wondering if this would work for me to knowing and trusting that it does. All I have to do is to keep on asking.

Summary of Chapter 4

I'll level with you. I don't really understand how these Attraction principles work. I just experience regularly that they work for me and they work for my clients. But just as a racing driver doesn't need to be able to build a formula one car to be a great driver you don't need to be a physicist to benefit from the Laws of Attraction. Here's a short formula for how to work with them:

1. Get clear on what it is you do want (often by deciding what you don't want and then focusing on the positive opposite). Whatever you do, avoid stating your goals in terms of what you don't want. Focus on bad stuff and you'll get it!
2. Ask for what you want. Spend time experiencing the feelings of having what you do want now.
3. Trust that the process works. If you believe it doesn't work then of course it won't – for you.
4. Work on raising your own vibration so that you are a match for the 'feeling place' of whatever you want to attract.

Chapter Five – The Inner Work – Who Are You Being?

In this chapter we're going to focus on you, and your awareness of who you are, of your attitudes and beliefs. You can have the best marketing plan in the world, but if you don't feel confident about putting it into action, how effective is it going to be? If you're spending your time and energies on areas other than where your talents lie then is that the best use for them?

From an attraction viewpoint, working on each of these steps will result in you feeling better about yourself, which means your energy will be vibrating at a higher level, making it easier for you to attract whatever you want.

So, let's get started!

Step 16. I know my own strengths and am proud and grateful for them

We are all made up of a unique mixture of talents and strengths. Similarly we all have other areas that we are not so strong in. Our culture, led by our fantastically critical education system, tends to concentrate on remedying the weaknesses, rather than celebrating and building on our strengths. Doesn't it make sense to build on the things where we've already got a head start? If you think of people who are really successful, they work on what they're already good at, honing their skills to a really high level in a usually narrow area of specialism. The Attraction Marketing system is built on the premise of focusing on what you enjoy doing, which in most cases will be those areas that you are naturally strong in. I bet you already know what they are, don't you?

Attraction in Action:

1. Identify your strengths. A task that is often easier said than done, especially as we are not often encouraged to name them. Here are some suggestions to get you started:
   - Ask family and friends, or colleagues to tell you what strengths they observe in you.
   - Compile a list of those areas you believe you're strong in.
   - Buy a copy of 'Now, Discover Your Strengths' by Marcus Buckingham – this book includes access to a web based questionnaire, developed by the Gallup Organisation, that identifies your top five strengths.
2. Decide how you can capitalise on these strengths in your business.
3. Modify your marketing plan if necessary to accommodate these new discoveries.

This is another area I resisted like mad because I was brought up to believe that it was a bad thing to think too highly of yourself. Modesty was valued higher than excellence. Singing your own praises, blowing your own trumpet or showing off, even to yourself, were frowned upon. Instead it was much more acceptable to work on myself to improve that great big list of weaknesses I had.

A word to the wise: if you catch yourself saying, "I should", what you mean is, "I don't really want to, but someone else thinks I ought to". It's worth taking the time to reflect on who that somebody is, and whether their opinion really matters at this moment in time. Often it'll turn out to be the nebulous 'they' who think you should do the ironing instead of lounging in your garden on the first sunny Saturday for months.

Back to those weaknesses – I could have easily written you a full description of each of them, and how they disadvantaged me from running a successful business, but identify a single strength? Not so easy…

And knowing that I wasn't an outgoing extrovert meant I didn't want to subject myself to the torture of the networking meeting, or that realising I tend to procrastinate meant I put off making warm calls, let alone cold ones. So by focusing on my weaknesses, I didn't attempt the things I believed I'd fail at. So I read another email or two, or went along to another "cosy coaches" meeting, and generally didn't get on with the real business of growing my business.

I was forced out of this state, reluctantly, by a coach that I began working with who insisted on me taking a personality profile at the beginning of our work together. When I picked up on the negative comments from that, and wondered how I was ever going to be successful with those qualities, she introduced me to the Marcus Buckingham book, 'Now, Discover Your Strengths' and the on–line assessment.

I was amazed by what I learnt from this. Those things that are so simple for me that I'm surprised everyone else doesn't find them as easy as falling off a log, are my strengths. They matter. They are part of what makes me unique. Knowing this was a real 'aha!' moment. Once I realised my strengths a world of possibilities opened up for me. By using these strengths as the cornerstone of how I went about my business building, I could be successful by being and building on who I already am rather than worrying about what I'm not.

Step 17. I take responsibilities for my outcomes

Most of us are brought up by our parents and schooling to take responsibility for our actions. As a society we have laws that tell us what acceptable and unacceptable actions are, police that ensure we abide by those laws, and a judiciary system that dispenses justice and punishment for breaking them. So most of us do take responsibility for our actions most of the time.

Taking responsibility for our outcomes is another matter though. In terms of our behaviour in this area, everyone falls somewhere on a spectrum between the neurotic personality at one extreme, who takes responsibility for everything, even if it's got nothing whatsoever to do with them, to the other extreme, where it's never that person's fault in any way.

This lack of responsibility shows up in life and business in various ways:

- ✗ I was too busy working with clients to do any other marketing, and now I've got no work.
- ✗ Well, the market is declining at the moment, so it's difficult trading conditions for us.
- ✗ I'm not skilled in selling, so I'll put off calling that person I met at a networking meeting – they probably won't want to hear from me anyway.
- ✗ I don't really have any plans for life so I'll just take what comes.

All of these, and all the other variations they come in, are excuses of one sort or another for why you failed to achieve what you really wanted. If you don't take responsibility for what you get then someone else will. And guess what they've got planned for you? Not much.

Attraction in Action:

1. Do any of the above excuses sound familiar? Have a good long hard look at yourself to discover if you have a tendency to make excuses for not getting the outcomes you want that are within your control.
2. Write down your answers to the following questions: If I take responsibility for my outcomes, what have I got to do differently in my life? What would I be doing that I'm not currently doing?
3. Create an Action Plan from your answers.

Boy, this was a huge area of learning for me. I knew that my father was someone who never considered anything to be his fault, he was the kind of person who'd hit a stationery hedge that, "came out of nowhere!" I was also aware that my son found it hard to think about outcomes and could be easily seduced by the 'play now, leave your homework to the last minute' message. And I thought it fascinating that this character trait had skipped an entire generation in me. I was totally responsible for my outcomes, thank you very much, just not very successful at building a coaching business.

It took an amazing coach I was working with, after several months together, to take a deep breath and say to me that in her opinion I was totally irresponsible, I took no responsibility whatsoever for becoming a success and that if I didn't make changes immediately I never would be. Ouch! that hurt! But then, the truth often does.

And so she gave me this exercise to do too. Here's what I wrote:

"If I take responsibility for my outcomes, what have I got to do differently in my life? What would I be doing that I'm not currently doing?"

- ✓ I would stop making excuses to myself and the world about why I haven't done something – why I failed.

- ✓ I would learn how to look "beyond the brick" – i.e. look in anticipation of the reward that is waiting for me after I've done a particular task I don't want to do or am scared of doing.
- ✓ I would be willing to set targets, even if I haven't got any clue how I am going to achieve them. The world would not end if I didn't achieve them.
- ✓ I would stop viewing failure as a terrible thing, but view it as a lesson to be learned from.
- ✓ I would face up to discomfort and fear, rather than avoiding it, knowing that I will have grown through the experience.
- ✓ I would not be put off from doing what I saw as a necessary but boring task.
- ✓ I would alter my thinking from, "I'll do the best I can, but of course, I'm only little old me and it's not my fault if I don't succeed" to, "To achieve what I want, what I have got to do is x, and what I need to do that is y – and maybe I'll need to get help on this from z".
- ✓ I would let go of the fear that if I were responsible for all my outcomes, I would not be able to cope with the workload.

Doing this exercise, and the action plan that came out of it, was a real turning point for me. My coach warned me that I would have to guard against the old ways slipping back in, as it is far harder for us to think in new ways than in old ones. Especially when we become tired or under stress – it's a matter of our physiology. The brain finds it quicker and easier to send messages down the existing network of neural pathways rather than to create new ones that we build up by thinking and acting in new ways.

If you are someone who grapples with responsibility, I'd encourage you to spend a good deal of time on this exercise and get support to help you establish truly responsible ways of being and working.

Step 18. I know my areas of weakness, and am taking steps to strengthen these

Now this may sound a strange step following after Step 16, which was advising you to build on your strengths, but bear with me, and it should be an easy step for you to do.

'Strengthening' your weaknesses means finding ways of working around them, rather than investing a lot of time and effort to build talents where they don't exist. There may be a minimum level to which you need to increase your performance in a weak area, but your efforts will be better placed expanding your strengths. For example, if maths isn't a strong point, the minimum you might decide you need is to be able to understand profit and loss accounts (i.e. are you making any money?) but that the book–keeping itself can be delegated to someone who revels in it.

Attraction in Action:

1. Identify your areas of weakness. Be gentle to yourself as you do this, putting all mental whips away. Look back to the strengths list and remind yourself how great you are first!
2. Think about each area you've identified, and ask yourself the question "What is the worst that could happen to my business because of my weakness in that particular area?" Pick the 3 outcomes that would have the worst effect on your business, and brainstorm ways of getting around them.
3. Then make and implement your action plan.

As you can imagine, I'd already got my long list of weaknesses compiled long before this stage. The interesting thing for me was that I realised many of my apparent weaknesses didn't have a great deal of impact on my business at all! The fact that I can't touch my toes or sing in tune is totally irrelevant to being a coach and just because I could never get my head around algebra doesn't mean I can't read and understand a profit and loss account.

I realised from the exercise that unless I got my head around marketing, the worst that would happen to my business was that it wouldn't exist any more, so that was an area that definitely needed working on.

Step 19. I am comfortable with asking for support in areas where it's required

You may need support in one of several areas and your business will benefit if you are willing to ask for it. Asking for help where needed shows that you are really committed to making your business as successful as possible.

If you are self–employed, working on your own can feel quite isolated, especially if you're home based. Do you know of professional groups in your area that you could attend, or maybe you could set up a regular conference call with others in your field?

Working on your own can mean that you lack the opportunities to bounce ideas around and to gain broader insights. You could choose to counter this by setting up your own mastermind group, a small group of business people in unrelated professions who you trust and admire. The group would meet regularly to help each other grow their businesses with the thinking of the group being greater than the sum of all the parts. Alternatively, you could choose to hire a coach who will help you clarify and expand your thinking.

It can also be harder to keep the motivation going when you haven't got anyone but yourself to be accountable to. Again, this is an area where working with a coach reaps huge benefits. There is nothing like telling someone else that you're going to get something done by a certain time to ensure that you do! Alternatively, you could set up a telephone based support group to keep you on track with tasks.

Your professional development is another area that can suffer without some form of outside support. How do you keep your skills honed and up to date with the latest developments in your profession?

If you're not an expert in areas such as accountancy or law, how can you be sure that you're meeting the current legislation? How can you gain access to the knowledge you need?

Attraction in Action:

1. Think about your business – where do you know you could benefit from some support?
2. Take an action step towards setting this support up for yourself. It's okay to ask for help.

I've found support is one of the unquantifiable benefits I gained once I became involved in networking groups where professionals in various fields are happy to share their knowledge. I also gained greatly from bouncing ideas around with other coaches when I was first in business. A word of warning though – I found I was using my time chatting with other coaches as a means of not getting on with the marketing work I knew needed my attention. Long lazy lunches in the pub bemoaning the difficulty of finding clients with other unsuccessful people is not what I mean by asking for support.

Step 20. My actions are not limited in any way by my fears

Now this is where you get to meet your gremlin, that little voice in your head that says things like, 'You might fail', 'Who do you think you are, pretending you can run a business?', 'You've never succeeded before, why do you think you will this time?' and so on. I bet you know the voice I'm on about, don't you? All of us have a gremlin, it is the voice of people from our past, and it basically wants to keep us safe, by not letting us taking any risks. But of course it can stop us from moving forward in the direction we want. The key is to 'make friends' with your gremlin, so that it can act as a friendly mentor rather than your own worst enemy!

Attraction in Action:

1. Become aware of the gremlin's voice and what it says to you.
2. Personalise your gremlin, give it a name – some examples I've heard are Hot Air Horace, Silly Sally, Pessimistic Pete. The aim is for you to realise and accept that this is not you putting the dampers on your actions, but the voice from the tape of your past. All those people you came across who gave you messages about your perceived inadequacies will have fed it.
3. When it talks to you, thank it for its input and tell it that you're an adult now, and that you intend to proceed with your plans.
4. Notice over time how the gremlin gets quieter and shows up less frequently.

My gremlin was called 'Bob Up Bob' and he took the shape of one of those baby toys that comprise a blow up rubber body with a weight at the bottom, that when you knock it starts to fall over and then rights itself again – it just bobs back up again. 'Bob Up Bob' could be various sizes as he appeared from my shoulder, sometimes just a little chap, and sometimes, as he started his chatter, he would grow and grow, until he was towering over my head.

And as you can tell by my use of the past tense, he really doesn't visit very often at all now!

Step 21. I have let go of my limiting beliefs

I'm not talking about religion or politics here, or even about the Laws of Attraction, I'm talking about the beliefs that we all hold about how the world works and who we are in the world.

We have to have these beliefs to make sense of our world, and to be able to operate in it successfully. When you wake up in the morning, imagine if you didn't believe that you were in the same room you went to sleep in last night. Or that you're still who you were yesterday. Imagine if you weren't sure whether the floor was going to be solid enough to take your weight. You'd be exhausted by breakfast time, and the day would be over before you got anywhere.

So we build up a set of beliefs from childhood onwards that help us in our daily life. Unfortunately, we can often end up with some that become outdated, suitable for when we were defenceless children, but no longer appropriate as adults. Or we'll end up with others that simply don't support us to develop our potential. These are the 'limiting beliefs'. The ones that hold us back from success.

Some examples of these limiting beliefs are:

- I am stupid
- I don't have a right to say what I think
- I don't deserve success
- I'm too young
- I'm too old
- My ideas don't matter
- I can't handle this
- I am trapped with no choice or power
- My feelings don't matter
- I can't change things
- I'm not lovable
- I'm not attractive
- It is up to me to make everyone's life right
- I'm not a leader

- ✗ You have to find the right answer
- ✗ It isn't possible
- ✗ You can't have it both ways
- ✗ Change is always difficult and takes a long time

These beliefs are not real, they only exist within the confines of your head, but you are guided by them nonetheless. You look for evidence that fits in with your beliefs, thus reinforcing them, and you filter out and just don't notice any evidence to the contrary.

Because your beliefs are not concrete facts, but ideas that you hold to be true, you can choose to change them to beliefs that are more relevant to who you are now. You can pick and choose beliefs that support you to develop your potential and you can rid yourself of old ones instantaneously.

Attraction in Action:

1. Think about where you feel you're holding yourself back in some way, and identify a belief you have about who you are and how the world works that is preventing you from moving forward in this situation.
2. Write down what holding on to this belief does for you, how does it serve you?
3. Write down how this belief makes you behave, on a variety of levels: physical, intellectual, emotional, spiritual.
4. Write down the evidence you have for it being true.
5. Write down the evidence you have for it being false.
6. Create a new belief that's the positive opposite of your old belief.
7. If the new belief is true, what would you do differently? Write this down and create and implement an action plan based around it. Act as if it was true.
8. Write down all the evidence you gain to support the new belief being true.
9. Keep practicing new ways of reinforcing this new belief.
10. When you've built this new way of thinking, go back to the beginning and identify and change another limiting belief.

The tricky part of identifying beliefs in my experience is the fact that I just took them for granted as being true, and so found it required conscious effort to uncover them. What I found helpful was to take the list I wrote to my coach about what I would have to do differently if I were to take responsibility for my outcomes, and to decide based on that what I currently believed and what the positive opposite would be.

For example, the first item on my Do it Differently list was 'I would stop making excuses to myself and the world about why I haven't done something, why I failed'. The belief I found behind this was 'It's not my fault if things don't work out', and I could find masses of evidence to support this one. Turning it around to the positive opposite gave me two new beliefs – 'If I do or don't do something, that's down to me, and me alone' and 'I have a choice about what I do'.

Step 22. My work is an expression of who I truly am

We each have a number of core 'values', those qualities that are the essence of who we are. Values in this sense include such things as beauty, elegance, honesty, compassion, pleasure, leadership, and many more. Values are not like our needs, which can be satisfied. We will always feel more fulfilled when the way in which we live allows us to fully express our values.

So if our work is based around our values as well as our strengths, which we identified earlier on then we will feel more fulfilled, which is a very attractive quality!

Attraction in Action:

1. Remember a time when you were feeling on top of the world, fully fulfilled, even if fleetingly. What was going on for you then? What qualities of life were you expressing at that time? Note these down.
2. Remember a time when you were feeling really low, and examine what was not showing up in your life at that time. This will give you clues as to which qualities are important to you for your sense of fulfilment. Note these down.
3. Compare your two lists. It is likely that what was missing from your life in list 2 shows up in list 1; this is a good indication that it is one of your core values.
4. Do you feel that your work allows you to express your values? If not, what would need to change for you to feel more fulfilled in your work?

Once you know your core values, you have a lodestone for judging any life decisions against by asking yourself whether your intended course of action will allow your values to show up or not. For instance, if you're someone who has a strong value of beauty, taking a job in an unattractive environment would tend to make you deeply unhappy, whereas that environment might hardly be noticed by someone who didn't have beauty as a value.

When I did this exercise, I uncovered that my values were independence and freedom, making a difference for others, learning, variety and new adventures. You can see why I revel in running my own business as a coach, especially now I'm working with the attraction marketing system.

Summary of Chapter Five

You've now completed your 'inner work' which will support you in being someone who not only has an effective attraction marketing system for their business, but someone who is using their potential to the full.

If you did the exercises in this chapter you should easily be able to answer yes to the following:

- ❑ I know my own strengths and am proud and grateful for them
- ❑ I take responsibility for my actions and for my outcomes
- ❑ I know my areas of weakness and am taking steps to strengthen these
- ❑ I am comfortable with asking for support in areas where it's required
- ❑ My actions are not limited in any way by my fears
- ❑ I have let go of my limiting beliefs
- ❑ My work is an expression of who I truly am

Chapter Six – Becoming More Attractive

There are a number of steps you can take that have an impact on how attractive you are. By that I mean how you deliberately work with the Laws of Attraction to increase your ability to attract to you what you want. And they are steps worth taking anyway regardless of how far up the scale of acceptance you've moved. Even if you're not ready to accept the Laws of Attraction as true yet they'll all make you feel happier and enjoy life more.

So, let's get started!

Step 23. I have a positive attitude to life

Remember the findings of Dr Wiseman's statistical survey of 'lucky' people? One of their four common characteristics was that they had a positive outlook on life. Why does this bring them 'luck'? Because they are looking out for the positive, expecting that things will work out well for them, and in line with the Laws of Attraction, this is what tends to happen for them.

Each of us has a way of looking at life that is just natural for us. It will fall somewhere between the two extremes of 'Life Totally Sucks' to 'Life is Pure Heaven'. Your viewpoint will have been influenced by your basic personality, your experience of life to date, and your family and cultural background. Wherever you fall on the attitude continuum, the good news is that you can shift your attitude towards the more positive end of the scale.

Attraction in Action:

1. Think about your general attitude to life and ask yourself "Where on the scale between 'Life Sucks' to 'Life is Heaven' do I fall?"
2. Reflect on why your attitude is as it is. Has it been shaped by your own life experiences, or did you inherit it from your family? Does it come with the territory of your cultural background or was it born with you?
3. How does your current attitude work for you? Does it contribute towards you feeling generally less or more excited with life?
4. If you decide that your outcomes would be better if you could shift your attitude to a more positive one, start today:
    a) Start by listening and looking out for how other people's attitudes show up in the way they approach things.
    b) Next, begin listening to your own thoughts and

words so that you build your awareness of just how positive or negative you are.

c) Then if you hear yourself being negative, think afterwards, how could you change what you said into a more positive version?

d) Your responses to life are based on habit, so just as you formed the original habit through repetition, so you can create a more supportive habit by repetition of the desired behaviour. Plus, as a positive attitude produces more pleasurable feelings in you than negativity does, these good feelings can be the spur to keeping on building up the habit. Good feelings really are vital for the success of the attraction process.

Step 24. I am able to look for the gift in difficult situations

To phrase this another way, as the saying goes, "If life gives you lemons, learn how to make lemonade."

Many people are deterred by setbacks, sometimes to the point where they give up. They can find themselves dwelling on their difficulties and feeling sorry for themselves. Take my friend Susanna for example – at a regular networking meeting she received a referral for a piece of paid work that would showcase her talents to nearly 100 other businesses, all of them potential clients. This was a major opportunity for her. At the same meeting however, she discovered that a job she had quoted for had gone to someone else in her field. She was so upset by this 'failure' that she began considering leaving the networking group entirely.

But if you have the mindset that is looking for the opportunity in every circumstance that befalls you, it enables you to make the best of even the most difficult situations. This will keep you moving forward towards your goals, although possibly by a different route than you originally had in mind.

Attraction in Action:

1. Think of occasions when life did give you a lemon – what was your response? Did you feel hard done by, or maybe a failure? Or was your response to think OK, how can I turn this situation around? If it was the latter, well done, you're holding a strong hand in the attraction game, but if your tendency is to feel discouraged, read on.
2. Looking back on that difficult situation, brainstorm ideas of how you could have turned it around to your advantage until you have listed at least 10 different ways to find a gift. Allow the ideas to be as weird and wonderful as possible – the aim is to open your mind to all the possibilities that abound.
3. Now repeat this brainstorming technique on a few more disappointing situations from your life. You are practicing flexing your creative muscles so that next time a lemon comes your way, you'll be able to produce a choice of possible responses that will help you make delicious lemonade!

Step 25. I am grateful for all the good things in my life, large and small

Many people moan and groan about all the things, both large and small, that go wrong in their lives yet they'll simply take it for granted when things go well. The Laws of Attraction state that what you focus on is what you get, so it follows that if you can increase your ability to first notice and second hold your focus on the good things that come to you, you'll receive more good things. The first step towards doing this is to develop an 'attitude of gratitude'.

Attraction in Action:

1. Make the decision to keep a gratitude journal as well as a success log. At the end of every day, write a list of three things that have happened in your day or that are in your life that you're grateful for (they need not be connected with your business).
2. Develop the habit of watching out for successes and things to be grateful for throughout the day, from getting a new client, to finding the last parking space in a busy car park, to some money arriving, to the sun shining.
3. Observe closely how your luck seems to get better as you continue to say thank you for things – and remember to be grateful for that improved luck.

My Mother would know this step as Counting Your Blessings, which seems to be a habit that a lot of people have dropped, and would be incredibly beneficial to them if they'd just start it up again.

This step is really where a lot of change in attitude started for me and it eventually led me to the Laws of Attraction. I began keeping my gratitude journal long before I'd even heard of coaching. It was at a time when I was feeling pretty negative about life in general, and for a while my entries were a reflection of what was going on for me at the time.

1. My house didn't get destroyed by an earthquake today, so that's good.
2. I haven't committed murder today, so that's to be thankful for.

I discovered that, once I'd established the habit, I could make this gratitude list mentally as I fell asleep, and ended up having a much more refreshing and restful night's sleep than I was used to when I fell asleep with my head full of the trials and tribulations of the day. My tendency had been to focus on the one event that had gone wrong during the day and to totally ignore all the things that had gone right.

Gratitude was one of the first of the Attraction principles that I started to read about, and it gave me my first experiences of deliberate creation. I read that being grateful for finding a parking space made it more likely that you would find one another day. Ever the sceptic, I set out to try this out, to see what happened, and I discovered it to be true. Now if I'd taken the attitude of, 'I know this won't work', that would have been my experience too, but I approached it with an open mind, with a sense of wondering. I am now amazed and incredibly grateful to regularly find my parking space waiting for me in the busiest of car parks.

Step 26. I only do work that I feel good about and marketing that I enjoy

Does the work you're doing give you a real buzz, a real sense of exhilaration and fulfilment? Does the work you dream of for the future also give you those strong positive feelings? If it does, you'll discover you can draw towards you more of this positive energy through the workings of the Laws of Attraction, which just like the Law of Gravity are operating around us all the time, whether we're aware of it or not.

If however your work leaves you feeling dissatisfied, or you're feeling despondent because you don't have enough clients, according to those same Laws of Attraction, you will attract more of that same feeling to you. As you focus on the lack of clients you attract a similar lack of clients. As you focus on your sense of dissatisfaction with the work you're settling for, you'll attract yet more of that dissatisfied feeling into your life.

Are you at networking events feeling like a fish out of water, cringing inside at the thought of speaking with people? Or are you feeling scared about cold calling and frustrated with your lack of results? Again, your energy is getting lower, you're vibrating at a more negative level, and as night follows day, you'll be attracting similar feelings into your experience.

To change these situations around you need to either change how you feel about how you're spending your time (the 'fake it 'til you make it' approach) or change how you're spending your time.

Attraction in Action:

1. Think about the work that you do for your clients and rate the 'buzz' level that it gives you on a scale of 1 (very little joy from it) to 10 (you just love doing this work, it leaves you feeling totally fulfilled, and you would happily do it all day long even if you weren't paid for it – although of course you are amply rewarded for it).
2. If all your work rates a 10 score, congratulations! If it's lower than a 10, what would you need to change in order to score 10 out of 10?
3. If an area of your work brings you less than a score of say 6, question why you're doing it at all. You may answer, for the money, in which case I would ask you the following question: If you knew that you really can attract to you only the work that you love to do and the clients you love to work with, but that that process is being slowed down by your somewhat negative feelings about the work you're doing, what is it costing you to carry on doing that work?
4. Based on your findings make yourself an action plan and take a step forward towards raising your work satisfaction levels today.

Step 27. I look out for synchronicities

The word 'synchronicity' was first used by the psychologist C.G. Jung in 1952, but the concept has been in existence for centuries. He defined synchronicity as:

"A meaningful coincidence of two or more events, where something other than the probability of chance is involved."

F. David Peat, in his book 'Synchronicity – The Bridge Between Matter and Mind' wrote:

"As Jung has earlier pointed out, it is the nature of synchronicity to have meaning and, in particular, to be associated with a profound activation of energy deep in the psyche. It is as if the formation of patterns within the unconscious mind is accompanied by physical patterns in the outer world. In particular, as psychic patterns are on the point of reaching consciousness then synchronicities reach their peak; moreover, they generally disappear as the individual becomes consciously aware of a new alignment of forces within his or her personality.

"Synchronicities are therefore often associated with periods of transformation; for example, births, deaths, falling in love, psychotherapy, intense creative work, and even a change of profession. It is as if this internal restructuring produces external resonances or as if a burst of 'mental energy' is propagated outward into the physical world."

Attraction in Action:

A simple step. Just notice when 'meaningful coincidences' occur and note them in your success journal. You can then look back on them and notice what came out of them and also notice if they increase in number as you are 'working creatively' on developing your attraction marketing system. Notice what significance they had for you.

I would expect that most of us would have some experience with 'meaningful coincidences', where you bump into just the person you needed to meet at that time in a totally unexpected place or through a strange set of circumstances.

My friend Carole told me an amazing story that illustrates the concept. She was called down to visit her father urgently in hospital in his home town, where she was brought up but hadn't lived for many years. While she was with him at the hospital he suddenly died. She was really upset, especially as she hadn't realised quite how ill he was and had travelled down on her own to see him. Feeling bereft, she went into the hospital cafeteria and sat down with a cup of coffee. After a few minutes, she felt a tap on her shoulder, only to discover that sitting at the next table were her two best friends from school thirty years ago. They never normally used the hospital cafeteria, but one of them had to attend for a blood test and had arranged to meet the other one there for lunch. They were delighted to see Carole and were able to comfort her and stay with her until her husband arrived some hours later.

My personal experience is that, as you focus on regularly imagining your future success and taking steps to increase your attractiveness, these occurrences do indeed increase. They are not usually quite as dramatic as Carole's story, but each of them does take you forward in some way towards your vision.

Step 28. I respond to opportunities and let go of the outcome

One of the qualities of an attraction marketing system as opposed to a traditional one is that it feels much more effortless. Attraction draws things towards you, rather than you having to push and strive to achieve them. If it's feeling too hard, find another way of doing things.

However, relying on attraction does impose some responsibilities on you if it's to prove successful as the basis of your marketing programme. One responsibility you have is to keep on working at feeling better and better, so that you raise your energy levels and attract higher circumstances to you.

Another is to respond to opportunities that appear through synchronicity for you. You can check with yourself through your intuition whether they are right for you (I'll show you how shortly) and then spring into action quickly. Dithering about your course of action once you have chosen to embark on the path of attraction marketing will keep you stuck.

To be prepared to respond promptly requires you to develop your ability to trust that the process will work for you. If you're in doubt about it, that very doubt will decrease your energy levels and your results. Some people say that an acronym of the word TRUST stands for 'Totally Relying Upon Spirit Timing'.

Whatever your thoughts about spirituality, I feel the relevant thought for me here is that it's wise to accept that sometimes things happen that we have no control over.

Once I know that I have done absolutely everything within my power to achieve what I want then my best course of action is to let go of worrying about the outcome. If it works out how I want it, that's great, and if it doesn't, that's fine too.

Attraction in Action:

1. Notice whether your marketing feels more effortless than it did. Notice where you feel you are pushing or striving, and choose a course of action that seems to have less resistance to it.
2. Notice how you react to opportunities that arise. Are you cautious about responding to them? Do you consider every opportunity intuitively as well as rationally before deciding your response?
3. Notice where you are able to trust that things will work out however they're meant to, and where you're very clear that you must get a certain result. Notice what the difference is for you when the various results happen.
4. If you were able to be unattached to the outcome, what difference could that make for you? What benefits would that give you?

As an ex–persistent worrier, making the change (gradually) to someone who is on the whole unattached to outcome is very welcome. It means you get a better sleep and a more enjoyable laid–back life.

I recommend it!

Step 29. I listen for, and act on, my intuitive hunches

Listening to their intuition was one of the characteristics of the 'lucky' people identified by Dr Wiseman, and is a natural skill that is often undervalued in today's scientific and logical age. However once you allow yourself to really develop your natural instincts, you'll find that intuition is an inner sense that can bring you as much valuable information as your other senses can.

Intuition is at work when you suddenly think, "I must phone so and so", someone you haven't thought of for ages, and when you ring them, you were just the person they needed to hear from at that time. When this happens you're then part of their synchronous event.

Intuition is at work in the 'brainwaves' that come to you, often when you're doing something completely unrelated like having a shower or weeding the garden – these are the flashes of inspiration that lead you to new approaches and ideas.

Intuition adds another layer of knowing to your rational decision making process. It can be used as a check with your inner self that the decision you've made on a logical basis sits comfortably with your instincts. On the other hand, if you are someone who finds decision making hard, who can reach a stage of 'analysis–paralysis' then using your sense of intuition allows you to access your inner wisdom and get unblocked.

Attraction in Action:

1. Decide to actively increase your intuitive abilities. Listen out for the unexpected thoughts about contacting someone you haven't spoken to for a while, and note down their response when you ring them.
2. Keep notepads around your house and office, so that when a 'brainwave' strikes you, you can capture it, no matter the time and place. Then decide how you can act on it later. Again, note down the results so that you can build up an awareness of how your intuition is helping you succeed.
3. When you've got to make a decision, take a few moments of peace and quiet to ask yourself what you should do. Then transfer your attention to your heart, focus on the beating of your heart in your chest, and keep it there for a little while. As you develop your ability to quieten your mind enough to maintain your focus, you'll find that the answer to your question will come quietly into your mind. Build up your trust in this ability by using it on small daily decisions before moving on to larger life ones. As ever, note down the results of your experiments, so that you gradually build a body of evidence for the process. This will increase your trust in it and thus your chances of being in the right place at the right time.

Intuition is definitely a skill that can be developed, or maybe a better way of saying it would be that it's a skill that can be re–accessed. I know from my own experience that it can be squashed over time by the fear of making a mistake and by the need to be absolutely certain before moving forward. I remember that intuition was one of the modules on my coach training, and that I told the teacher that I didn't have any at all. I did slowly learn to hear the quiet inner voice, and more importantly, to trust that I could take action on what I heard, that it was okay to risk making a mistake. The real mistake was in doing nothing at all.

Step 30. I create a regular number of quiet spaces in my life for reflection or meditation

In today's world of information overload, your brain is often working flat out. If you think of your mind as a pot on the stove, the surface of the contents of the pot are often bubbling and boiling away incessantly.

Remember the comment about brainwaves. They often come to you when you're focused on something else, when your brain is idly daydreaming. The most successful ideas don't often come when you force them to arrive, nor is there any space for them to come when your mind is a whirl of thought. To increase the frequency of those flashes of brilliance, you need to increase your ability to quieten your mind, to allow the surface of the pot to become calm and still. It is in these 'quiet moments' that the best ideas will bubble up from your inner self.

Attraction in Action:

1. Make the decision that you want to learn how to quieten your mind so that you can make space for those inspired thoughts to arrive.
2. Decide on the 'how'. You can choose to learn how to meditate or maybe you prefer to take quiet walks, go swimming, paint a wall. The method itself doesn't matter, what is important is that you choose a repetitive activity that allows your mind to float freely away but is engaging enough to prevent your mind going in to overdrive.
3. Decide on the 'when'. Like developing any other ability, learning how to quieten your mind takes regular practice, but will bring you great rewards.
4. Start right now. Once you've read this section, take a few moments to ask your intuition what your first action now should be.

I gradually discovered how to still my mind through doing vini yoga, which I really didn't want to do. My doctor insisted, because I was suffering from neck ache due to poor posture. I slowly began to access the ability to stop thinking for initially very short periods of time, a few seconds, which then gradually built up to longer and longer periods.

I found that as my mind stopped racing around, I was able to think more clearly about the things I chose to think about, such as formulating workable plans. I also found that I was more able to stay in the present, rather than churning over memories of the past or worrying about events in the future.

If you're busy thinking in an unstructured way, you're not noticing what's around you, you're not 'taking time to smell the roses'. And it's through smelling the roses, by savouring the moment, that you increase your ability to be happy. Being happy has a much higher energy level than worrying about events past or present. Therefore, from an Attraction perspective, the more you can still your mind and be in the moment, the higher your energy vibration and the greater your ability to attract what you want.

Summary of Chapter Six

Fantastic work. You should now be able to answer yes to the following:

- ❑ I have a positive attitude to life
- ❑ I am able to look for the gift in difficult situations
- ❑ I am grateful for all the good things in my life, large and small
- ❑ I only do work that I feel good about & marketing that I enjoy
- ❑ I look out for synchronicities
- ❑ I respond to opportunities
- ❑ I listen for and act on my intuitive hunches
- ❑ I create a regular number of quiet spaces in my life for reflection or meditation

Chapter Seven – Into the Future

You have now completed the last of the Attraction in Action steps, which I hope have inspired you to continue your journey of discovery and success! What you now have is the basic framework for attracting all the clients you want – you just have to use it.

In this final section of your Attraction Marketing journey, I'm going to ask you to take a step off the path and sit down on the roadside for a short while to take a well–deserved pause for rest and reflection.

The reflection I'm going to ask you to do is in five parts:

1. Where are you now?
2. Where have you come from?
3. How to celebrate?
4. What was your experience of the journey?
   and
5. Which way forward?

So, let's get started!

Reflection One: Where are you now?

Congratulations for reaching the end of this book. If you've been taking action on all the Attraction in Action steps, I wonder what has changed for you already?

- ✓ How much of your vision has started to be attracted to you?
- ✓ How many new clients have you attracted over the period you've been working through these steps, and how many of them are truly ideal?
- ✓ What are the results, both tangible and intangible, that you have gained from reading this book?

There has been a great deal of effort required of you so far, some of which I know from experience can take several weeks or even months to fully implement, so you may feel that you're very much just getting started – and that's just fine. You've reached the end of this book, and found the beginning of your new marketing approach. Use this book as a map as you journey forward.

Reflection Two: Where have you come from?

Often you can be so busy moving forward that you forget to take a little time out to stop and look back over your shoulder at where you came from. It's often only then that you can truly appreciate just how much you have achieved along the way.

In part one of this book, you took an assessment to show you where your starting point was in terms of your attraction marketing system. How has your score increased from then to today? In case you haven't been marking it off as you go along, below is the assessment again so that you can check your updated score.

Tick the box only if the statement is always true for you.

- ❑ I am in a position of 'visibility' to my ideal clients
- ❑ I am very clear about the benefits I offer my clients
- ❑ I can explain these benefits succinctly and memorably to people I meet
- ❑ I know exactly which clients I can help the most and why
- ❑ I am aware of my unique selling point in my marketplace
- ❑ I add additional value to all my clients
- ❑ I have a basic understanding of selling skills
- ❑ I can identify my ideal client and have a clear picture/description of them
- ❑ I know what I want my business to be like in 1, 3 and 5 years time
- ❑ I have a written marketing plan
- ❑ I set goals and targets for my business marketing and review them regularly
- ❑ I monitor results regularly and adjust my marketing plan accordingly
- ❑ I allocate regular planning time to my marketing

- ❑ I take consistent, persistent action on my marketing to avoid the yo–yo effect
- ❑ I know how I will feel about my business in 1, 3 and 5 years time
- ❑ I know my own strengths and am proud and grateful for them
- ❑ I take responsibility for my actions and for my outcomes
- ❑ I know my areas of weakness and am taking steps to strengthen these
- ❑ I am comfortable with asking for support in areas where it's required
- ❑ My actions are not limited in any way by my fears
- ❑ I have let go of my limiting beliefs
- ❑ My work is an expression of who I truly am
- ❑ I have a positive attitude to life
- ❑ I am able to look for the gift in difficult situations
- ❑ I am grateful for all the good things in my life, large and small
- ❑ I only do work that I feel good about and marketing that I enjoy
- ❑ I look out for synchronicities
- ❑ I respond to opportunities
- ❑ I listen for and act on my intuitive hunches
- ❑ I create a regular number of quiet spaces in my life for reflection or meditation

______ Total Ticked

So, how far has your journey been since the beginning of the programme? What are you pleased and grateful for? Which leads you straight on to Reflection Three.

Reflection Three: How to Celebrate?

I really ask that you take this step very seriously, whether you have been able to implement all the steps of the programme and are now enjoying working with the ideal number of ideal clients, or whether you feel you're still on a learning curve.

Celebrating your successes bolsters your self–esteem, increases your confidence in your abilities and makes you feel good. As you know, the Laws of Attraction state that what you focus on is what you get, so as you celebrate, you increase your levels of gratitude, positive energy and emotion, all of which allow more of what you want to manifest for you.

So how are you going to celebrate?

Reflection Four: What was your experience of the journey?

Although the Laws of Attraction have been operating unbeknownst to man from time immemorial, it is only very recently that people have realised just how much their attitudes and thoughts affect the results of their actions. So you are in a way pioneers on this particular journey.

As your guide who is walking at most a very short way in front of you (and even that may well not be the case) I am curious how you have found the journey, so that I can update the map for those that come after you. If you'd like to contact me at the address at the end of the book, I'd love to hear your experiences.

Reflection Five: Which way forward?

So, you've come so far – what's the way forward like for you?

Is your route ahead clear and uncluttered? Great, I wish you well on your journey, and would love to hear about your experiences.

Is the path ahead a little foggy, or are there obstacles in the way that seem insurmountable? Were there some steps on the programme that you found easy and others that you are struggling with, or resisting tackling? What would help you? What's the action step you could take today that would move you forward?

And so you've come to the end of this book. My intention in producing it was to give you a basic map for working with the Laws of Attraction, combined with some powerful marketing techniques and habits, so that you can produce the results you desire. I'm aware that it is only an introduction, and leaves many questions unanswered, but I hope that it has prompted your curiosity to explore further.

Whichever path you choose from here, I hope that you have enjoyed your introduction to the Attraction Marketing system, and have found it helpful and valuable in attracting the ideal number of ideal clients to you.

I wish you all that you truly desire.

Best Wishes
Annie Meachem, ACC

About The Author

Annie Meachem is a professional certified coach who helps creative entrepreneurs attract clients so they can spend more time doing what they love and less time marketing and runs regular workshops in Attraction Marketing. She also works with individuals who want to feel whole and happy and that they're living a meaningful life.

For further details contact:
Annie Meachem, Trellis Coaching
0845 456 9382 / +44 (0) 1243 545010 (from outside UK)
email: annie@trelliscoaching.com / website: www.trelliscoaching.com

Printed in the United Kingdom
by Lightning Source UK Ltd.
116872UKS00001B/35

9 780954 568153